REPENTANCE AND CONFESSION

REPENTANCE AND CONFESSION IN THE ORTHODOX CHURCH

John Chryssavgis

HOLY CROSS ORTHODOX PRESS
Brookline, Massachusetts 02146

Second Printing 1996

© 1990 Holy Cross Orthodox Press
Published by Holy Cross Orthodox Press
50 Goddard Avenue
Brookline, Massachusetts 02146

Library of Congress Cataloging-in-Publication Data

Chryssavgis, John.
Repentance and confession in the Orthodox Church
By John Chryssavgis.
p. cm.
Bibliography. p.
Includes index.
ISBN 0-917651-56-1 (pbk.)
1. Confession--Orthodox Eastern Church.
2. Repentance--Orthodox Eastern Church.
3. Orthodox Eastern Church--Doctrines.
I. Title. BX378. C6C48 1988
265' .6--dc 19

In loving memory of
and respectful gratitude to
Professor Nikos Nissiotis

CONTENTS

PREFACE

Wherever confession is practiced, it is often carried out in a mechanical fashion and without much spiritual preparation. And since the only reason for confession is to achieve reconciliation and "reintegration into the Body of Christ, which has been torn usunder by sin," proper preparation is an absolute must. Too often, however, many Orthodox Christians do not know how to prepare themselves adequately. Moreover, helpful materials to serve as a guide are often lacking. This need has been admirably filled by the Reverend John Chryssavgis, a young, brilliant Patristic scholar from Australia.

It is not surprising, therefore, that after offering a short but insightful essay on confession and repentance in the Orthodox tradition, Fr. John presents in translation, excerpts from forty-two different Fathers and theologians of the Orthodox Church — ranging from Clement of Rome to Archimandrite Aimilianos of Simonos Petra of the Holy Mountain. These readings assist the reader to delve deeply into the subject of confession and repentance and are splendid help for spiritual meditation.

The volume ends with the Service of the Penitents (Confession) which itself is a storehouse of spiritual wealth and guidance. In short, Fr. John has performed a very valuable service to all English-speaking Christians with his splendid book on Confession and Repentance. May it have the success it deserves.

Fr. N. Michael Vaporis, Ph.D.
Professor of Byzantine and
Modern Greek History

1

INTRODUCTION

Confession is in decline and repentance is misapprehended. The decline and the misapprehension cannot be easily qualified, but they are unmistakable at least inasmuch as they are considered to be no more than incidental practices in the life of the Church today. The "traditional" way of thinking of sin and forgiveness has collapsed among a growing number of Christians. Nothing less than a theological and pastoral renewal is necessary in order to rediscover the living meaning of repentance and confession.

The degeneration is often attributed to secularization. Yet secularization should not be seen, in a scapegoat fashion, as merely an external enemy. It acts from within the Church. Even those actively involved in church life suffer from formalism caused by the established patterns of religious practice. There is a need to appeal to the deepening of repentance and confession as spiritual realities rather than their imposition as obligatory customs. It is only in a realization of the nature of sacramental life that repentance acquires its significance as a way of renewal and reconciliation in Christ.

Repentance is indeed an act of reconciliation, of reintegration into the Body of Christ, which has been torn asunder by sin. For "if one member suffers, all suffer together" (1 Corinthians 12.26). "Therefore, confess your sins to one another . . . that you may be healed" (James 5.16). The whole Church expresses a search for repentance in the repeated

3

words of the Psalmist, commonly known as the "miserere" (Psalms 50). It is through the faith of the community that the individual is readmitted and forgiven. "When Jesus saw their faith he said, 'man, your sins are forgiven' " (Luke 5.20; cf. Matthew 9.2 and Mark 2.5). "Justification" in the New Testament does not mean a transaction – a kind of deal; and repentance defies mechanical definition. It is a continual enactment of freedom, a movement forward, deriving from renewed choice and leading to restoration. The aim of the Christian is not even justification but a re-entry by sinner and saint alike into communion in which God and man meet once again and personal experience of divine life becomes possible. Both prodigal and saint are "repenting sinners."

Repentance is not to be confused with mere remorse, with a self-regarding feeling of being sorry for a wrong done. It is not a state but a stage, a beginning. Rather, it is an invitation to new life, an opening up of new horizons, the gaining of a new vision. Christianity testifies that the past can be undone. It knows the mystery of obliterating or rather renewing memory, of forgiveness and regeneration, eschewing the fixed division between the "good" and the "wicked," the pious and the rebellious, the believers and the unbelievers. Indeed, "the last" can be "the first," the sinner can reach out to holiness. Passions are conquered by stronger passions; love is overcome by more abundant love. One repents not because one is virtuous, but because human nature can change, because what is impossible for man is possible for God. The motive for repentance is at all times humility, unself-sufficiency – not a means of justification for oneself, or of realizing some abstract idea of goodness, or of receiving a reward in some future life. Just as the strength of God is revealed in the extreme vulnerability of His Son on the Cross, so also the greatest strength of man is to embrace his weakness: "for my strength is made perfect in weakness. Most gladly therefore will I render glory in my infirmities, that the power of Christ may rest upon me" (2 Corinthians 12.9). To be flawed is the illogical, perhaps supernatural characteristic of humanity in which one encounters God.

The Greek term for repentance, *metanoia*, denotes a change of mind, a reorientation, a fundamental transformation of outlook, of man's vision of the world and of himself, and a new way of loving others and God. In the words of a second-century text, *The Shepherd of Hermas*, it implies "great understanding,"[1] discernment. It involves, that is, not mere regret of past evil but a recognition by man of a darkened vision of his own condition, in which sin, by separating him from God, has reduced him to a divided, autonomous existence, depriving him of both his natural glory and freedom. "Repentance," says Basil the Great, "is salvation, but lack of understanding is the death of repentance."[2]

It is clear that what is at stake here is not particular acts of contrition, but an attitude, a state of mind. "For this life," states John Chrysostom, "is in truth wholly devoted to repentance, *penthos* and wailing. This is why it is necessary to repent, not merely for one or two days, but throughout one's whole life."[3]

Any division within oneself or distinction between the "time to repent" and the "rest of one's time" is, in the language of the Church, attributed to the demons. The role of these demons is extortionate, offensive — *"diavallo,"* the root of the word "devil," means to tear asunder.[4] We cannot be deprived of true repentance or diverted from its path by the deception of demons. Yet the demons can work through virtue, working to produce a kind of spurious repentance. By nature we are destined to advance and ascend spiritually, but the demons divert the course by simulating advance in the form of a fitful movement, a wobbling from side to side, like crabs. One can test the quality of repentance by ascertaining whether it is fleeting or fluttering. Inconstancy and inconsistency are a danger signal; lastingness is auspicious. One is being tempted by the demons when one is caused "at times to laugh, and at other times to weep."[5]

THE TWO DIMENSIONS OF REPENTANCE

Divine Initiative

Repentance is not a self-contained act: it is a passing over, a *Pascha* from death to life, a continual renewal of that life. It consists of a reversal of what has become the normal pattern of development, which is the movement from life to death. To experience this reversal in repentance is to have tasted of the glory and beauty of God; it is the mark of man's presence before God in the abundance of His mercy and of God's presence before man in the abyss of his weakness: "Set Your compassion over against our iniquities, and the abyss of Your lovingkindness against our transgression."[6] It is the awareness of God's beauty that makes one realize the chasm that separates one from His gratuitous grace. The initiative belongs to God, but presupposes man's active acceptance, which is a way of perpetually receiving God within the heart, of God being embodied within man, of divine incarnation. Here God calls man, and man responds to God and in doing so gains salvation and life abundant: "sorrow working repentance to salvation not to be repented of" (2 Corinthians 7.10). In repentance it is man's total limitation and insufficiency that is placed before God, not simply particular wrongdoings or transgressions.

The "dialectic" of beginning and end underlying repentance is important. Every manifestation of life has an eschatological dimension, even while, paradoxically, repentance gives rise to restoration, to a return to man's original state. Everything tends towards and expects the "end," even while being a matter of the here and now. To repent is not merely to induce a restoration of lost innocence but to transcend the fallen condition.[7] Indeed the greater the fall, the deeper and more genuine the repentance and the more certain the resurrection. Man is "enriched" by his experience even if it has been crippling and tormenting. The Fathers appear to express greater love – almost a preference – for the more sinful person, inasmuch as thirst for God increases in proportion to the experience of one's debasement and abasement (Romans 5.20).

The word for "confess" in Greek (ἐξομολογοῦμαι, ὁμολογῶ) does not bear the contemporary meaning peculiar to it. When we say "confess" we imply that we accept, recognize or witness an event or fact. But this is not the original meaning. The point is not of admitting, more or less reluctantly, a hitherto "unrecognized" sin, but an acceptance of and submission to the divine Logos (*exomologesis*) beyond and above the nature and condition of man.[8] It is this Logos, the Word of God, that man seeks to regain, or rather to commune with. To confess is not so much to recognize and expose a failure as to go forward and upward, to respond from within to the calling of God. Created in the image and likeness of God, man bears before himself and in himself that image and likeness. In repenting he does not so much look forward as reflects and reacts to what lies before and beyond him.

However, repentance is also a way of self-discovery: "Open to me the gate of repentance."[9] *Metanoia* is the gateway to oneself, to one's fellowman, and to heaven. It leads inwards, but it also leads outwards by leading inwards. The world ceases to rotate round the self and begins to gravitate towards the other — the divine and the human other. Sin has the opposite effect. It blocks the way both inwards and outwards. To repent and to confess is to break out of this restriction, "to accept with joy," in Isaak the Syrian's words, "the humility and humiliation of nature," to transcend and to recover oneself. The world thereupon ceases to rotate around "me" and begins to gravitate towards the other, centering on God. Then, everyone and everything no longer exist for myself but for the glory of God, in the joy of the Resurrection. One is then able to comprehend more clearly the positive dimension of even sin, suffering, death, the devil and hell. Then, one discovers the depth of love crucified, the presence of the Lord in our midst — even "when the doors are shut" (John 20.19,26). One is not, however,

demanded to love God from the outset, but rather to know
that "God so loved the world, that He gave His only begotten
Son" (John 3.16). Nevertheless, the love of God is implicit in
His very nature. God Himself is the Archetype of divine love.
When John the Theologian says that "God is love" (1 John
4.8,16), love is seen as an established ontological category
of both divinity and humanity in His likeness. In fact, the
beauty and loving freedom of the human person is, in the
words of Nicholas Berdiaev, God Himself. It is He, "the creator of all . . . who out of extreme erotic love moves outside
Himself . . . burning with great goodness and love and eros."
It is He who is "the fullness of erotic love."[10] And it is this
supreme love that moved God to create human nature in
His image and likeness. "As Lover, He creates; and as Loved,
He attracts all towards Him."[11] "As a mad Lover He desires
His beloved human soul," says Saint Nilos.[12] "Herein is love,
not that we loved God but that He loved us (1 John 4.10).

The response to this ineffable outpouring of love is none
other than its acceptance. Repentance thereby acquires a
different dimension to mere dwelling on human sinfulness,
and becomes the realization of human insufficiency and
limitation. Repentance then should not be accompanied by
a paroxysm of guilt but by an awareness of one's estrangement from God and one's neighbor. Why, after all, does one
not partake of Holy Communion after committing sin? Not
for punishment, but surely because sin itself is a denial of
communion. The paradox of God's love is that one is only
saved again through communion. Although God is constantly
being chased away by humanity, yet He returns day after
day in the Liturgy;[13] in the words of the Psalmist, "the
mercy of God runs after us all the days of our lives . . . for
His mercy endures forever" (Psalm 22.6, and 135). God is not
only at the end of the journey of repentance but also at the
beginning (Revelation 1.8), and Christ is the Way (John 14.6).
One seeks, then, Him whom one already possesses; and the
voyage is an unceasing arrival as well as a never ending
departure. Man in all his sinfulness is loved by God if he

can just keep moving towards God. When one *does* fall, if one only cries out with confidence, the fall is not into nothingness but into the arms of God stretched open once and for all on the Cross.

Human Response

"*Penthos*" is the conditioned sorrow of a repentant soul, adding sorrow upon sorrow each day, like a woman suffering in childbirth."[14]

Repentance, as has been noted, is not a mere incident or stage through which one passes and then leaves behind; rather it is an attitude which colors one's whole life and for which, at the same time, one must struggle continually. It is a way of life, and as such a way of transfiguration, in which man's heart and mind continuously receive illumination by the Holy Spirit. It is a continuous pathway, at least in this life, a perennial striving, an all-embracing motion and not merely an occasional emotion. Repentance is ultimately a gift of the Holy Spirit who transforms the heart of the human person, and not a fruit of individual effort or anguish.

Whether related to this continuity and endurance or to the depth of moral sensitivity involved, for the Fathers of the Church there is an intimate link between repentance and tears. There are other criteria,[15] but grief is paramount, and its intensity is proportionate to the depth of repentance. "Truly you are blessed, Abba Arsenios, for you wept for yourself in this world! He who does not weep for himself here below will weep eternally hereafter; so it is impossible not to weep, either voluntarily or when compelled through suffering."[16] Gregory the Theologian believed that everyone must weep. He even identified repentance with tears, whatever other ways of expressing it there may be: "All must shed tears, all must be purified, all must ascend."[17] Symeon the Theologian is even more definite: "Remove tears and with them you remove purification; and without purification no one is saved."[18]

The word *penthos* (mourning) has the same root as *pathos*

(passion): both stem etymologically from the verb "to suffer." A Christian speaks of worthy suffering, of subsuming
suffering in God, just as passion and mourning are subsumed
in God. There is suffering in compunction (*katanyxis* =
pricking), which also causes tears. "Joyful sorrow" trans-
figures this suffering and pain through grace. *Penthos* consists in mourning for the loss of God's presence; it makes for
sorrow at His absence and thirst for Him. "Passion or suffering for God gives rise to tears."[19] Man is in a state of bereavement, and the Church Fathers and liturgical hymnology
speak of Adam sitting opposite paradise in mourning over
his bereavement and estrangement from God. The *Makarian
Homilies* say that man must "weep his way back" to paradise.[20] But tears — a concomitant and a culmination of repentance — are also a turning point in homecoming, a pledge
of return, and a firstfruit of its joy. The longing for return
from exile is also an anticipation of the glory to come. Tears
demonstrate the frontier between the present and the future.

The tradition of the Christian East gives special promi-
nence to the "gift of tears."[21] The tradition can be traced to
the New Testament, through the Desert Fathers, to John Klimakos, through to later times, with Symeon the New Theologian standing out as one of its most important witnesses.
"Blessed are they that mourn, for they shall be comforted"
(Matthew 5.4). Tears are primarily "up to God," and only
derivatively "up to us." There is a thirteenth-century French
tale "Le chevalier au Barizel" according to which the knight
was supposed to fill up a barrel with water; he travels all
over the world to do this, but the water always passes
through the barrel. Seeing that his efforts achieve nothing,
he weeps, and one teardrop is sufficient to fill the barrel.
Tears bespeak a promise, and they are also proof of hope
fulfilled, of sins forgiven. But there is a time to weep and
a time to rejoice, although the one flows into the other. There
is a *kairos,* "a season and a time" (Ecclesiastes 3.1) for each
divine gift, and this *kairos* is the time in which God acts,
calling us to participate in His action. Tears are a way and

a consequence of purification through repentance; the ultimate goal is transcending light and delight.

THE SACRAMENT OF CONFESSION

A Christian, at any rate an Orthodox Christian, views repentance as a dynamic act of responsibility to God, but also to other men. It is not pining away in narcissistic self-reflection, even while implying self-knowledge and self-examination. Sin itself is a relational act — a break in the "I-Thou" relationship. It concerns my relationship with another person. When the prodigal son "came to himself" in the Gospel parable (Luke 15), he did so in relation to his father: "I will arise and go to my father, and will say to him, 'Father, I have sinned against heaven and before You' " (v. 18). We repent in the face of God; and we repent in communion with others, in the Church. Repentance in the early Church was in fact a solemn public act of reconciliation, through which a sinner was readmitted into church membership. Even in Buddhism, monks regularly confess their sins publicly before Buddha and the congregation; the phenomenology is the same as in the Church, even if the theology or ideology is different. Sin (and evil) divides, repentance conciliates, confession affirms the conciliation. Outside the community, outside the Church repentance would settle into guilty gloom, dulling the spirit or even driving to despair: *metanoia* turning into paranoia.

Confession, too, takes place within the Church. It is not a private procedure, a treatment of some guilt-ridden individual on an analyst's couch. It is not based on an admission of guilt and certainly cannot be reduced to a feeling of guilt, of liability for conduct contrary to norms and laws which render a person subject to punishment. It is related to what is deepest in man, to what constitutes his being and his relation with other human beings as well as with God. It is a sacrament — "the visible form of an invisible grace" (Saint Augustine), re-establishing a bond of union between God and man, between man and man. This is why confession also takes place within prayer because it is there that

a personal relationship in all its intensity is realized both
with God and the entire world. As such, confession and
prayer are not merely technical terms but means and opportunities offered by the Church for overcoming sin and
death. Repentance is indeed the cause and consequence of
prayer, being the highest and fullest foundation for and form
of prayer. "True prayer," according to Saint Anthony, "is that
in which one forgets that one is praying,"[22] and genuine repentance enables one to forget oneself and simply long for
God, who is present in the very depth of repentance. For it
is "before Him alone that one sins" (Psalm 50.3-4) − this is
the personal or relational aspect of both sin and repentance.

The supreme act of communion is the eucharist, the communal sharing of bread and wine, symbolizing sacrament-
ally the reconciliation to come and the reconciliation already
achieved in the here and now. Repentance and confession as
sacrament seals man's change of direction from disruption
to reconciliation. An examination of the early forms of confession shows that they are derived from community services and even liturgies. Origen explicitly stresses the significance of the eucharist for the forgiveness of sins.[23] Later
services for confession developed undoubtedly from community rites closely related to the eucharistic celebration,
or else to the monastic offices of matins or compline.[24]
Since forgiveness of sins involves reconciliation in and
through the eucharist, the eucharistic prayer contains penitential elements as immediate preparation for communion.

In early Christian times the exhortation of James served as
a foundation for the sacrament of repentance: "Therefore confess your sins to one another, and pray for one another, that you
may be healed" (5.16). Confession was regarded as a form of repentance and regeneration (Matthew 3.6; Mark 1.5; Acts 19.18).
The actual ritual aspect of repentance was a direct result of
such apostolic testimony, at first in the form of confession before the entire Church and, subsequently, before a spiritual father.[25] Nevertheless, the earliest *order* of confession is of rela-
tively late origin (tenth century), and is ascribed to John the

Faster, Patriarch of Constantinople.[26] This text may well be the source of later Greek and Slavonic services of confession.

The communal, sacramental aspect of confession was more apparent in the early Church when penance constituted a public act rather than an individual episode. It was only after the fourth century that private confession was more widely practiced. But even then penance did not have the legalistic and clericalistic character which it acquired later. In fact, very few Church Fathers refer even to absolution as a formal procedure, although such silence does not necessarily mean that absolution in some form or other did not exist. It is the reduction of sin to a punishable legal crime, an act of law-breaking inviting a penalty that is almost wholly absent in patristic literature.[27] "Have you committed a sin?," asks Saint John Chrysostom, "then enter the Church and repent of your sin . . . For here is the Physician, not the Judge; here one is not investigated but receives remission of sins."[28]

Unfortunately confession at times undermines and even replaces the genuine inner repentance of a Christian: people feel "entitled" to communion after confession. This contradicts the true nature of repentance. It is a result of the sacrament being narrowly and juridically reduced to "absolution." Scholarly theology tended to transpose the concept of sin, repentance and forgiveness into a forensic idiom, and placed the emphasis on the power of the priest to absolve. In the Orthodox Church, the priest is seen as a witness of repentance, not a recipient of secrets, a detective of specific misdeeds. The "eye," the "ear" of the priest is dissolved in the sacramental mystery. He is not a dispenser, a power-wielding, vindicating agent, an "authority." Such a conception exteriorizes the function of the confessor and of confession which is an act of re-integration of the penitent and priest alike into the Body of Christ. The declaration "I, an unworthy priest, by the power given unto me, absolve you" is unknown in the Eastern Orthodox Church. It is of later Latin origin and was adopted in some Russian liturgical books at the time of the domination of Russian Orthodox

theology by Latin thought and practice.[29] The idea served
to bring confession into disrepute, turning it into a procedure
of justification and exculpation in respect of particular punishable offenses. Forgiveness, absolution is the culmination
of repentance, in response to sincerely felt compunction.
It is not "administered" by the priest, or anybody else. It is
a freely given grace of Christ and the Holy Spirit within the
Church as the Body of Christ.

A word must be said about "general" confession, as distinct from a face-to-face confession between penitent and
priest. General confession, in certain circumstances, could
be a living model of repentance as a communal act, involving the whole body of the Church and as such manifesting
the very essence of confession.[30] But it is not strictly a sub-
stitute for personal confession, involving intimate self-examination on the part of the penitent and possible guidance on
the part of the confessor. Altogether, the function of the
priest should not be ignored or minimized. "All who have
experienced the blessing of having as their confessor one
imbued with the grace of true spiritual fatherhood," writes
Bishop Kallistos Ware, "will testify to the importance of the
priest's role. Nor is his function simply to give advice. There
is nothing automatic about the absolution which he pro-
nounces. He can bind as well as loose. He can withhold absolution – although this is very rare – or he can impose a
penance (*epitimion*), forbidding the penitent to receive Communion for a time or requiring the fulfilment of some task.
This, again, is not very common in contemporary Orthodox
practice, but it is important to remember that the priest possesses this right . . . Not that the penitence should be regarded as punishment; still less should it be viewed as a way
of expiating an offense . . . We do not acquire 'merit' by fulfill-
ing a penance, for in his relation to God man can never claim
any merit of his own. Here, as always, we should think
primarily in therapeutic rather than juridical terms."[31]

The most significant effect of confession is indeed due
neither to the penitent nor to the priest, but to God who

heals our infirmities and wounds. It is not a matter of a let-off, a clearance; it has the force of healing, of making the penitent whole. As such it is a gift from God which man must be open to receive, and learn to receive: "Let us apply to ourselves the saving medicine of repentance; let us accept from God the repentance that heals us. For it is not we who offer it to Him, but He who bestows it upon us."[32] It is significant that the Greek for confession, *exomologesis*, implies not only confession but also thanksgiving (cf. Matthew 11.25; Luke 10.21): "I shall confess/give thanks to the Lord with my whole heart, and tell of all His wonders" (Psalm 9.1).

Reference has already been made to the cloud of *guilt* which at times shrouds the sacrament of confession. It is by no means a theoretical question, for guilt is part of the tragedy experienced by many people, whether in their personal lives or in the face of the appalling sufferings and misery – mental, physical, social – which afflict the world at large today and for which we all share the responsibility and the guilt. But in the specific context of repentance and confession, guilt is a highly misleading concept, largely fostered by Western thinking.[33] It originates in a hypertrophied individualistic, self-regarding view of sin and salvation, and indeed of repentance with its attendant legalistically oriented penitential system. Orthodoxy always resisted legalism, whether in repentance or in confession, eschewing both undue confidence in man's achievement or merit and the overwhelming sense of guilt, which is the negative aspect of being centered on oneself and seeking for some means to propitiate God's wrath. By contrast with this God is seen to declare His love for men at their most unacceptable. It is God's identification with man and His loving acceptance of the worst that men can do that makes repentance and confession a way of rediscovering God and oneself, and thereby of being set on the road to full and loving relationship with God and with other men. There is no mention in Scripture of the word "guilt" (ἐνοχή), although there is the adjective "guilty" (ἔνοχος). Instead of "guilt" there is

"sin" (ἁμαρτία) – failure, loss, a break-up in relations, result-
ing in a kind of false consciousness. Even "ἐνέχομαι" implies
keeping fast within, cherishing, sharing, as distinct from being ashamed in the face of God who inflicts retributive
punishment.

Break in communication or communion can lead to path-
ological forms of guilt. But there is guilt born of a sense of
responsibility for others as well as for oneself, leading one
to an awareness of other people. The Christian view of man
is largely a social one. Where there is a breakdown in personal love, or a rise in institutionalism, one finds a thicken-
ing of the atmosphere of guilt. Its antidote is collective confession, communal prayer to "our Father." A saint might confess daily without fear of neurosis, because he is in constant
communion with God and man. Acknowledgment of one's
limitations leads to personal communion with God who
alone can erase sin: "I acknowledged my sin to You, and
I did not hide my iniquity. . . . Then You did forgive the
iniquity of my sin" (Psalm 32.5).

* * * * * *

Through the forgiveness of sins in confession, the past
is no longer an intolerable burden but rather an encourage-
ment for what lies ahead. Life acquires an attitude of expectation, not of despondency; and confession becomes the way
out of the impasse caused by sin. In this respect, repentance
is also an eschatological act, realizing in our very midst, here
and now, the promises of the age to come. Looking back-
wards would seem to imply the fate of Lot's wife (Genesis
19.26); "No one who puts his hand to the plow and looks
back is fit for the kingdom of God" (Luke 9.62). God Himself is revealed *before* us and walks *in front* of us. "One thing
I do, forgetting what lies behind and straining forward to
what lies ahead" (Philippians 3.13).

NOTES

[1]*Mandatum,* IV, ii, 2.

[2]*De Perfectione spirituali* 4 PG 31:636B.

[3]*De Compunctione I, i PG 47:395 and I, ix :408.*

[4]*Abba Isaias, Logos* 29,4.

[5]John Klimakos, *Ladder* 26:iii, 30 PG 88:1088C.

[6]First prayer of Kneeling Vespers at Pentecost.

[7]Cf. John Klimakos *Ladder* 4:125 PG 88:725D and 5:19 PG 88:780B.

[8]Cf. Archbishop Stylianos Harkianakis, 'Repentance and Confession' (in Greek: *Akropolis Newspaper,* Athens 10-4-80), p.6.

[9]Hymn of Great Lent.

[10]Dionysios, *De Div. Nom.* 4, 2 PG 3:712AB and Maximus, *Comm. in Div. Nom.*4, 17 PG 4:269CD.

[11]Maximus, ibid. and *De Amb.* PG 91:1260.

[12]PG 79:464.

[13]*De Charitate* 3, 2 in *Philocalia,* vol. 2.

[14]John Klimakos, *Ladder* 7:60 PG 88:813D.

[15]Cf. John Klimakos *Ladder,* 7:25 and 48 PG 88:805C and 809D.

[16]*Apophth.* Arsenios 41 PG 65:105CD.

[17]*Oration* 19,7 PG 35:1049D-1052A.

[18]*Catechesis* 29.

[19]Theodoret of Kyrrhos, *Philotheos Historia* XXX, Domnina 2 PG 87:1493AB.

[20]15, 17. Cf. *Kontakion* and *Oikos* of Cheesefare Sunday in *Triodion Katanyktikon* (Rome 1879), p. 105. Cf. also the prose-poem by Staretz Silouan in Archim. Sophrony, *Wisdom from Mt Athos* (London 1974), pp. 47-55.

[21]The doctrine regarding the 'gift of tears' is by no means unknown in the West, but it seems to have been accorded a higher place in the East, probably on account of the greater emphasis on the *heart* as a vessel of the Holy Spirit.

[22]In Cassian, *Conferences* 9, 31. Cf. also Evagrios, *De Oratione* 120 PG 79:1193B.

[23]*De Oratione* 28 PG 11:528-29.

[24]Cf. F. Nikolasch, 'The Sacrament of Penance: Learning from the East,' in *Concilium* 1, 7 (1971), 65-75.

[25]*Apostolic Constitutions* 8, 8-9; Gregory of Neocaesarea, *Canon*

XII. For confession before a spiritual father, cf. Socrates, *Ecclesiastical History* 5, 19 and 7, 16; John Chrysostom, *Sermon 4 on Lazarus* PG 48:1012.

[26]For a detailed description of this order, see N. Uspensky, *Evening Worship in the Orthodox Church* (S.V.S.: New York 1985), p. 227f.

[27]Cf. J. Meyendorff, *Byzantine Theology: Historical and Doctrinal Themes* (London 1974), pp. 195ff.

[28]*De Poenitentia* 3, 1 PG 49:292.

[29]Cf. A. Schmemann, *Confession and Communion: A Report* (New York 1972), pp. 13-16.

[30]St Nikodemos of the Holy Mountain (d. 1809) underlines the fact that it is God, not the priest, who forgives: Cf. *Exomologetarion* (9th ed. Venice 1885), pp. 77-78.

[31]Bishop Kallistos Ware, 'The Orthodox Experience of Repentance,' in *Sobornost/Eastern Churches Review* 2:1 (1980), 24-25.

[32]John Chrysostom, *De Poenitentia* 7, 3 PG 49:327.

[33]Timothy Ware, Eustratios Argenti: *A Study of the Greek Church under Turkish Rule* (Oxford, 1964), p. 20 ff.

THE SOURCES

CLEMENT OF ROME[1]

The Opportunities for Repentance Are Countless

Let us note what is good, what is pleasing and acceptable to Him who made us. Let us fix our eyes on the blood of Christ and let us realize how precious it is to His Father, since it was poured out for our salvation and brought the grace of repentance to the whole world. Let us go through all the generations and observe that from one generation to another the Master 'has afforded an opportunity of repentance' to those who are willing to turn to Him. Noah preached repentance and those who heeded him were saved. Jonah preached destruction to the Ninevites; and when they had repented of their sins, they propitiated God with their prayers and gained salvation despite the fact that they were not God's people.

The ministers of God's grace spoke about repentance through the Holy Spirit, and the Master of the universe Himself spoke of repentance with an oath: 'For as I live, says the Lord, I do not desire the death of the sinner, but his repentance.' He added, too, this generous consideration: 'Repent, O house of Israel, of your iniquity. Say to the sons of my people, Should your sins reach from earth to heaven, and be redder than scarlet and blacker than sackcloth, and should you turn to me with your whole heart and say "Father," I will heed you as though you were a holy people.' And in another place this is what He says: 'Wash and become

*Available translations have generally been adhered to in the "Sources," with certain modifications for the sake of uniformity; otherwise, the translation is original. Scriptural citations are from the Septuagint.

clean: rid your souls of wickedness before my eyes. Cease
from your wickedness, learn to behave well, devote yourselves to justice, rescue the wronged, uphold the rights of
the orphan and grant the widow justice. And come, let us
reason together, says the Lord; and if your sins are like pur-
ple, I will make them white as snow, and if they are like
scarlet, I will make them white as wool. And if you are willing and heed me, you shall eat the good things of the earth.
But if you are unwilling and do not heed me, the sword shall
devour you. For it is the mouth of the Lord that has spoken
thus.' Since therefore, He wanted all those He loved to have
an opportunity to repent, He confirmed this by His almighty
will.

So, brothers, since we have all been given no small opportunity to repent, let us take the occasion to turn to God
who has called us, while we still have One to accept us. For
if we renounce these pleasures and master our souls by
avoiding their evil lusts, we shall share in Jesus' mercy.
Understand that 'the day' of judgement is already 'on its way
like a furnace ablaze,' and 'the powers of heaven will dis-
solve' and the whole earth will be like lead melting in fire.
Charity, then, like repentance from sin, is a good thing. But
fasting is better than prayer, and charity than both. 'Love
covers a multitude of sins,' and prayer, arising from a good
conscience, 'rescues from death.' Blessed is everyone who
abounds in these things, for charity lightens sin.

Repentance Must Be Never-Ending

Genuine repentance according to God annihilates disobedience and abolishes darkness, illumines the eyes and
presents knowledge to the soul; leads man to salvation; and
that which he has not learned from men, he comes to know
through repentance.

While we are on this earth, let us repent. For we are but
clay in the hands of the artist. Just as the sculptor makes
a vessel: while the clay is in his hands, even if it falls, he
is able to remould it; but once it is placed in the furnace of

fire, he can do nothing more to it. Similarly, while we are in this world, let us repent with all our heart for the evils we have committed in flesh, so that we may be saved by the Lord while there is yet time for repentance. For after we have left this world, we are no longer able to confess or repent.

While there is time to be healed, let us offer ourselves to the healer God, giving Him as recompense our sincere-hearted repentance.

TERTULLIAN

A Second Baptism

[The devil's] poisons are foreseen by God; and although the gate of repentance has already been closed and barred by Baptism, still He permits it to stand open a little. In the vestibule He has stationed a second repentance, which He makes available to those who knock — but only once, because it is already the second time, and never more, because further would be in vain. Is not even this once enough? You have that which you did not now deserve; for you have lost what you had received. If the Lord's indulgence grants you the means by which you might restore what you have lost, be thankful for a benefit which has been repeated, and which has in fact been amplified. For it is a greater thing to restore than it is to give, since it is worse to have lost than never to have received at all.

If anyone becomes a debtor to the second repentance, certainly his spirit should not be immediately downcast and undermined by despair. By all means, let it be irksome to sin again; but let it not be irksome to repent again. Let it be shameful to be endangered again, but let no one be ashamed to be freed again. Medicine must be repeated for a repeated sickness. You will show your gratitude to the Lord if you do not refuse what He offers you again. You have

offended, but you are still able to be reconciled. You have
One to whom you may make satisfaction, and indeed He
is willing!

In regard to this second and single repentance, then –
since it is such a serious affair – so much the more laborious
is its examination. It is not conducted before the conscience
alone, but it is to be carried out by some external act. This
act, which is more usually expressed and spoken of by the
Greek word, is *exomologesis,* by which we confess our sin
to the Lord, not indeed as if He did not know it, but because
satisfaction is arranged by confession; of confession is repentance born, and by repentance is God appeased.

Positive and Ecclesial Aspects of Repentance

Confession is all of this, so that it may excite repentance;
so that it may honor God by fear of danger; so that it may,
by its own pronouncement against the sinner, stand in place
of God's indignation; and so that it may by temporal mor-
tification, I will not say frustrate, but rather expunge the
eternal punishments. Therefore, while it abases a man, it
raises him; while it covers him with squalor, the more does
it cleanse him; while it condemns, it absolves. Insofar as
you do not spare yourself, the more, believe me, will God
spare you!

With one and two individuals, there is the Church; and
the Church, indeed, is Christ. Therefore, when you cast
yourself at the knees of the brethren, you are dealing with
Christ, you are entreating Christ. In the same way, when
they shed tears over you, it is Christ who suffers, Christ who
implores the Father. When it is a son who asks, the request
is always more easily granted. How very grand is the reward
of modesty, which the concealing of our sin promises! If in
fact we conceal something from the notice of men, shall we
at the same time hide it from God? Are, then, the good opinion of men and the knowledge of God to be equated? Is
it better to be damned in secret than to be absolved in public?

'But it is a miserable thing thus to come to confession!' Yes, evil leads to misery. But where there is repentance misery ceases, because it is thereby turned to salvation.

Corruption in Human Nature Is Not Complete

Besides the evil in the soul which is brought in by the intrusion of an evil spirit, there is a prior evil which arises from the corruption of its origin, an evil in a certain sense natural. For, as we have said, the corruption of nature is another nature, having its own god and father, namely the author of the corruption. In spite of that, there is also in the soul that original good, the divine and genuine good, which is natural in the true sense. For what comes from God is not so much extinguished as obscured. It can be obscured, because it is not God: it cannot be extinguished, because it comes from God. So that, as a light, when its rays are interrupted by some obstacle, still remains, although it is not seen, if the obstacle be opaque enough: so the good in the soul, overcome by evil in proportion to the quality of that evil, either has its light obscured and is not seen at all, or sends out its rays when it finds a way through. Thus some men are very bad, and some are very good; and yet all souls are one genus; there is some good in the worst, some evil in the best.

CLEMENT OF ALEXANDRIA[3]

Look up at the Glory of God

True repentance is to be guilty no longer but to eradicate at once from the soul the sins through which death is known. For when these are revoked, then God immediately enters within man . . . To return to God is truly to cease from sinning, and to look back no longer.

He who approaches from here the angel of repentance will not need to repent afterwards, when he has left the body; nor will he be ashamed to approach the Savior with all His glory and attendance; nor again will he fear the fire.

It is of course good not to sin, but it is also good for the sinner to repent; just as it is very good to be healthy, but it is also good to heal the infirmity.

ORIGEN[4]

Mutual Forgiveness

But if we are unwilling to become gentler toward those liable to us, we shall experience what the man who refused to forgive his fellow servant a hundred *denarii* did. He had been previously forgiven according to the parable in the Gospel, and the master in anger made him pay what had been forgiven, saying to him, 'You wicked and slothful servant, should you not have had mercy on your fellow servant, as I had mercy on you? Throw him into prison till he pays all his debt' [cf. Matthew 18.33-34, 25.26]. And the Lord draws the moral, 'So also the heavenly Father will do to every one of you, if you do not forgive your brother from your heart' [Matthew 18.35]. Surely, those who have sinned against us must be forgiven when they say they repent, even if our debtor does this many times. For it says, 'If your brother sins against you seven times in the day, and turns to you seven times and says, "I repent," you must forgive him' [Luke 17.3-4]. And we are not harsh to those who do not repent. Rather, such people are evil to themselves, for he who ignores instruction hates himself [Proverbs 15.32]. Nevertheless, in the case of such people healing must be sought in every way possible, even for the person so completely perverted that he is not even conscious of his own evils and is drunk with drunkenness more deadly than that caused by wine, the drunkenness that comes from the darkness of evil [cf. Proverbs 20.1; Isaiah 28.1, 7; Matthew 24.49].

Sins Should Not Be Concealed

'That the thoughts out of many hearts may be revealed' [Luke 2.35]. There were evil thoughts in men, and they were revealed for this reason, that being brought into the open they might be destroyed, slain and put to death, and cease to be, and that He who died for us might kill them. For while these thoughts were hidden and not brought into the open they could not be utterly done to death. Hence if we have sinned we also ought to say, 'I have made my sins known to Thee, and I have not hidden my wickedness. I have said I will declare my unrighteousness to the Lord against myself.' For if we do this and reveal our sins not only to God but also to those who can heal our wounds and sins, our wickedness will be wiped out by Him who says, 'I will wipe out your wickedness like a cloud.'

ATHANASIOS THE GREAT[5]

Benefit from the Psalms

And it seems to me that these words become like a mirror to the person singing them, so that he might perceive himself and the emotions of his soul, and thus affected, he might recite them. For in fact he who hears the one reading receives the song that is recited as being about him, and either, when he is convinced by his conscience, being pierced, he will repent, or hearing of the hope that resides in God, and of the succor available to believers – how this kind of grace exists for him – he exults and begins to give thanks to God. Therefore, when someone sings the Third Psalm, recognizing his own tribulations, he considers the words of the psalm to be his own. And then when someone sings the Eleventh and Sixteenth, he considers how he is one making announcement in reference to his own confidence and prayer, and in the Fiftieth, how it is speaking the proper words of his own repentance.

You have sinned, and being ashamed, you repent and you ask to be shown mercy. You have in Psalm Fifty the words of confession and repentance.

JOHN CHRYSOSTOM[6]

The Boundless Love of God

Such is the love of God for mankind that He never rejects genuine repentance, but even if someone were to go beyond the limit of evil and desired to return from there to the way of virtue, He would receive and approach him, doing everything to guide him to his former condition. In fact, He is still more loving: for even if one did not show all repentance – even the very least – He would reward him much for the little repentance shown.

It is not He who ever turns away from us, but rather we who detach ourselves from Him.

If you have sinned and fallen, rise, arise please. For the good and loving Master who was put to shame by your sin is beside you and does not reject cohabitation with you. Give him your hand.

BASIL THE GREAT[7]

Now Is the Time for Repentance

This is the age of repentance, and that is the age of reward; this is the age of patience, and that the age of consolation.

They who believe in the Lord must first do penance according to the preaching of John and of our Lord Jesus Christ Himself; for they who do not penance now will receive a harsher sentence than those who were condemned before the time of the Gospel.

The present life is the time for penance and for the

remission of sins; in the life to come, the just judgement of retribution will take place.

GREGORY OF NYSSA[8]

An Example from the Old Testament

To the one who has lived without sin there is no darkness, no worm, no Gehenna, no fire, nor any other of these fearful names and things, as indeed history goes on to say that the plagues of Egypt were not meant for the Hebrews. Since, then, in the same place evil comes to one but not to the other, the difference of free choices distinguishing each from the other, it is evident that nothing evil can come into existence apart from our free choice.

Again the way led through the desert, and the people lost hope in the good things promised and were reduced to thirst. Moses again made water flow in the desert for them. When it is perceived spiritually, this account teaches us what the mystery of repentance is. Those who turn to the stomach, the flesh, and the Egyptian pleasures, after having once tasted the rock, are sentenced to be excluded from partaking in good things.

But they can by repentance again find the rock which they abandoned and again open the spring of water for themselves and again take their fill. The rock gives forth water to Moses who believed that Joshua's spying was truer than his opponents'; Moses who looked to the bunch of grapes which for our sake was suspended and shed blood, and Moses who by the wood prepared water to gush forth from the rock again for them.

But the people had not yet learned to keep in step with Moses' greatness. They were still drawn down to the slavish passions and were inclined to the Egyptian pleasures. History shows by this that human nature is especially drawn to this passion, being led to the disease along thousands of ways.

As a physician by his treatment prevents a disease from prevailing, so Moses does not permit the disease to cause death. Their unruly desires produced serpents which injected deadly poison into those they bit. The great lawgiver, however, rendered the real serpents powerless by the image of a serpent.

JOHN CASSIAN[9]

An Example of Confession

The old man said this to me: 'Take heart, my son. Without my saying anything, your confession has set you free from this captivity. Today you have won a victory over the adversary who had beaten you. Through your confession you have brought him down more completely than when you yourself were down as a result of that silence which he had prompted. No word uttered by you or by anyone else had stopped him, and until now you had given him the whip-hand over you. Even as Solomon said, "Because nothing is said against those doing wrong, the heart of the sons of men is so filled up that they do wrong" [Ecclesiastes 8.11]. Now because of this open denunciation of him, that most evil spirit will not be able to trouble you, and this most loathsome serpent will not take up a hiding place within you, for he has been pulled out into the light from your shadowed heart by this saving confession of yours.'

And the old man had scarcely finished these words when a lamp was lighted in my breast, and it so filled the cell with its sulphurous smell that its fierce stink barely allowed us to remain.

The old man continued: 'See! The Lord has given open proof to you of the truth of what I was saying. He wanted you to see the instigator of this passion expelled from your heart, before your very eyes, as a result of this saving confession. He wanted you to realize that by this open expulsion no further place would lie open within you for the enemy.'

It was just as the old man said. Through the power of this confession the grip of this diabolic tyranny was wiped out and forever laid to rest. The enemy never even bothered to revive in me the memory of this urge, and after this I never again felt myself moved by the wish to engage in stealing of this kind. We read this notion expressed so very well in Ecclesiastes: 'If the serpent does not have a whistling bite there would be no abundance for the soothsayer' [Ecclesiastes 10.11]. What he means there is the silent bite. That is to say, if one does not confess a diabolic idea or thought to some soothsayer, to some spiritual person well used to finding in the magic, all-powerful words of Scripture an immediate cure for these serpent-bites and the means of driving the fatal poison from the heart, there can be no help for the one who is in danger and about to perish.

We will most easily come to a precise knowledge of true discernment if we follow the paths of our elders, if we do nothing novel, and if we do not presume to decide anything on the basis of our own private judgement. Instead let us in all things travel the road laid down for us by the tradition of our elders and by the goodness of their lives. Strengthened by this routine a person will not only reach the summit of discernment, but he will remain completely safe from the snares of the enemy. For the devil drags a monk headlong to death by way of no other sin than that of submission to private judgement and the neglect of the advice of our elders.

All the skills and disciplines devised by human talent for the benefit of this temporal life can be laid hold of, observed, and understood, but only with the necessary help of some instructor. Now the spiritual life is unseen and hidden, open to only the purest heart. Here the fact of going wrong brings harm that is not of this world and that cannot easily be rectified. Rather, it causes the loss of the soul and everlasting death. So, then, how stupid it is to believe that only this way of life has no need of a teacher! Here the enemy to be encountered is not visible but is unseen and pitiless. Here the spiritual fight goes on day and night and is waged not against one or two but against countless hordes and is all the more dangerous for everyone because the enemy is more vicious and more secretive. And so the footsteps of our elders must always be followed with the utmost care and every thought in our hearts must be submitted to them, stripped of the cover of false modesty.

THEODORE OF MOPSUESTIA[10]

The Remedy for Sin

If we have committed a serious sin of any kind which implies rejection of God's will, we must abstain from Communion. But we must not allow ourselves to stay away indefinitely. No, indeed, we must rouse ourselves to repentance. We must not leave the healing of sins to themselves. God has given us the remedy of confession, according to the discipline of the Church. This is the treatment of sins that God had entrusted to the priests of the Church.

AUGUSTINE OF HIPPO[11]

A Personal Experience

And certainly from you , O Lord, before whose eyes the depth of the human conscience is laid bare, what in me could be hidden although I were unwilling to confess it to You? I could not then be hiding myself from You, but You from myself. But now when my groaning witnesses to my displeasure with myself, You shine out upon me and You are pleasing to me, loved and desired, so that I am ashamed of myself and renounce myself and choose You and, except in You, can please neither You nor myself. Whatever I am, therefore, O Lord, is laid bare before You. And the benefit I derive from confessing to You, I have stated. Nor do I confess with bodily words and speech but with words of the soul and the clamor of my thoughts which Your ear understands.

For when I am wicked, to confess to You is to be displeased with myself; but when I am good, to confess to You is not to attribute this goodness to myself: since You, O Lord, bless the just man, though first you convert him from ungodliness to justice. And so my confession, O my God, is made in Your sight silently and not silently. For although it makes no noise, it cries aloud in my heart. For if what I say to men is right, You have first heard it from me; but anything You hear from me, You Yourself have first said it to me.

Why should men hear my confessions as if they would heal all my infirmities? They are a race very curious about the lives of others, very slothful in improving their own. Why should they wish to hear from me what I am when they are unwilling to hear from you what they are? And when from me they hear my account of myself, how do they know that I speak truly seeing that 'no man knows what is in man but the spirit of man which is in him' [1 Corinthians 2.11]? But if from You they hear about themselves, they cannot say: 'The Lord is lying.' For to hear about themselves from you is simply to know themselves. And who knowing himself can say 'it is false' unless he himself is lying? But because 'charity believes all things' [1 Corinthians 13.7] (that is, among those whom it binds together to make one), I confess to You so that men may hear me, though I cannot prove to them that I am telling the truth; but they whose ears charity opens to me believe me.

Yet I ask you, my inmost Physician, to clarify for me what benefit I gain in doing it. For the confessions of my past sins (which You have forgiven and covered so much that You might make me happy in You, transforming my soul by faith and Your sacrament), when read and heard, stir up the heart lest it fall asleep in despair saying: 'I cannot,' and that it may awaken in the love of Your mercy and the sweetness of Your grace by which, when aware of his own weakness, every weak person becomes strong. And it delights good people to hear of the past evils of those who are now freed from them; they are delighted with the evils but only because they who were evil no longer are.

Then with what benefit, my Lord, to whom my conscience, more secure in Your mercy than in its innocence, daily confesses, with what benefit, I ask You, do I confess before You and also before men through this book not what I once was but what I now am? As to my confession of the past, I have both seen and recounted that. But as to what I now am, at this very moment of writing my confessions, there are also many people who desire to know this, those who know me and those who do not know me who have heard of me or from me; but their ear is not against my heart where I am whatever I am. They wish, therefore, to hear me confessing what I am within myself – which is beyond the reach of their eyes, ears, or understanding. Although they wish to believe, will they understand? That charity by which they are good tells them that in my confessions I would not lie, and that charity in them believes in me.

The benefit of confessing not what I have been but what I am is this: I confess not only before You , in a secret 'exaltation with trembling' (Psalm 2.11) and in secret sorrow with hope, but also in the ears of the believing sons of men, companions of my joy and partners in my mortality, my fellow citizens and fellow pilgrims, both those who have gone before and those who follow after, as well as my companions on the way.

For 'You, Lord, judge me,' because, although 'no man knoweth the things of a man, but the spirit of a man which is in him' [1 Corinthians 2.11], yet there is still something of man which even the spirit of man that is in him does not know, but You, O Lord, who made him, know everything about him. As for me, though in Your sight I despise myself and esteem myself but dust and ashes, yet I know something of You which I know not of myself. And certainly we see 'now through a glass darkly, not yet face to face' [1 Corinthians

13.12], and therefore, as long as I wander away from You, I am more present to myself than to You; yet I know that You are in no way subject to violence, whereas in my case I do not know what temptations I can and cannot resist. Yet there is still hope, because 'You are faithful, who will not suffer us to be tempted above that which we are able: but will with the temptation also make a way to escape, that we may be able to bear it' [1 Corinthians 10.13]. Therefore, I shall confess what I know of myself, I shall confess also what I do not know of myself, since what I know of myself I know by means of Your light shining upon me, and what I do not know remains unknown to me until in Your countenance 'my darkness be made as the noonday' [Isaiah 58.10].

THE DESERT FATHERS[12]

The Essence of Repentance, Revealed in the Radical Simplicity of the Desert

A brother asked Abba Agathon about fornication. He answered, 'Go, cast your weakness before God and you shall find rest.'

Abba Elias, the minister, said, 'What can sin do where there is penitence? And of what use is love where there is pride?'

Abba Theodore of Pherme said, 'The man who remains standing when he repents, he has not kept the commandment.'

It was related of a brother who had committed a fault that when he went to Abba Lot, he was troubled and he hesitated, going in and coming out, unable to sit down. Abba Lot said to him, 'What is the matter, brother?' He said, 'I have committed a great fault and I cannot acknowledge it to the Fathers.' The old man said to him, 'Confess it to me, and I will carry it.' Then he said to him, 'I have fallen into fornication, and in order to do it, I have sacrificed to idols.'

The old man said to him, 'Have confidence; repentance is possible. Go, sit in your cave, eat only once in two days and I will carry half of your fault with you.' After three weeks the old man had the certainty that God had accepted the brother's repentance. Then the latter remained in submission to the old man until his death.

He also said, 'The nearer a man draws to God, the more he sees himself a sinner. It was when Isaiah the prophet saw God that he declared himself a "man of unclean lips" ' [Isaiah 6.5].

A soldier asked Abba Mios if God accepted repentance. After the old man had taught him many things he said, 'Tell me, my dear, if your cloak is torn, do you throw it away?' He replied, 'No, I mend it and use it again.' The old man said to him, 'If you are so careful about your cloak, will not God be equally careful about His creature?'

A brother questioned Abba Poimen saying, 'I have committed a great sin, and I want to do penance for three years.' The old man said to him, 'That is a lot.' The brother said, 'For one year?' The old man said again, 'That is a lot.' Those who were present said, 'For forty days?' He said again, 'That is a lot.' He added, 'I myself say that if a man repents with his whole heart and does not intend to commit the sin anymore, God will accept him after only three days.'

He also said concerning Abba Pior that every day he made a new beginning.

A brother questioned Abba Poimen saying, 'What does it mean to repent of a fault?' The old man said, 'Not to commit it again in future. This is the reason the righteous were called blameless, for they gave up their faults and became righteous.'

Abba Poimen said that blessed Abba Anthony used to say, 'The greatest thing a man can do is to throw his faults before the Lord and to expect temptation to his last breath.'

It was said of Abba Sisoes that when he was at the point of death, while the Fathers were sitting beside him, his face shone like the sun. He said to them, 'Look, Abba Anthony is

coming.' Again his countenence shone with brightness and
he said, 'Look, the choir of apostles is coming.' His countenance increased in brightness and lo, he spoke with someone. Then the old men asked him, 'With whom are you
speaking, father?' He said, 'Look, the angels are coming to
fetch me, and I am begging them to let me do a little
penance.' The old men said to him, 'You have no need to
do penance, father.' But the old man said to them, 'Truly,
I do not think I have even made a beginning yet.' Now they
all knew that he was perfect. Once more his countenence
suddenly became like the sun and they were all filled with
fear. He said to them, 'Look, the Lord is coming and he's
saying, "Bring me the vessel from the desert!" ' Then there
was a flash of lightening and all the house was filled with
a sweet odor.

This is what they relate about Abba Sisoes when he became ill. The old men were sitting beside him and he spoke
to some of them. They said to him, 'What do you see, Abba?' He said to them, 'I see beings coming towards me, and
I am begging them to leave me a little while so that I may
repent.' One of the old men said to him, 'And even if they
allow you a respite, can you now profit by it and do
penance?' The old man said to him, 'If I am not able to do
that, at least I can groan a little over my soul and that is
enough for me.'

Abba Moses asked Abba Sylvanos, 'Can a man lay a new
foundation every day?' The old man said, 'If he works hard,
he can lay a new foundation every moment.'

A brother asked Abba Poimen what he should do about
his sins. The old man said to him, 'He who wishes to purify
his faults purifies them with tears and he who wishes to acquire virtues acquires them with tears. For weeping is the
way the Scriptures and our Fathers give us when they say,
"Weep!" Truly, there is no other way than this.'

He also said, 'The wickedness of men is hidden behind
their backs.'

A brother questioned Abba Poimen, 'What ought I to do

about all the turmoils that trouble me?' The old man said
to him, 'In all our afflictions let us weep in the presence of
the goodness of God, until He shows mercy upon us.'

A father once said, ' . . . Today, O Master, from this time
forward, receive me, as I repent and throw myself at Your
feet, desiring in future to abstain from every fault.' He continued, 'With these promises, I came out of the church, sure
in my soul that I would no longer commit any evil before
God.' At these words they all with one voice cried out to
God, 'How manifold are Your works, Lord, in wisdom have
You made them all' [Psalm 104.24]. So, as Christians, having learnt from the holy Scriptures and from holy revelations, let us know the great goodness of God for those who
sincerely take refuge in Him and who correct their past faults
by repentance, and let us not despair of our salvation. In
truth, as it was proclaimed by the prophet Isaiah, God
washes those who are dirty with sin, whitens them as wool
and as snow, and bestows the good things of the heavenly
Jerusalem on them; even as, in the prophet Ezekiel, God
has sworn by an oath to satisfy us and not to let us be lost.
'For I have no pleasure in the death of anyone,' says the Lord
God, 'so turn, and live' [Ezekiel 18.32][a].

An old man said, 'Every evening and every morning a
monk ought to render an account of himself and say to himself, "What have we not done of what God does not want,
and what have we done of that which God wills?" In this
way he must live in repentance. This is what it means to
be a monk, and this is how Abba Arsenios used to live.'

It was said of an old man that when his thoughts said
to him, 'Relax today, and tomorrow repent,' he retorted, 'No,
I am going to repent today, and may the will of God be done
tomorrow'[b].

Abba Anthony used to say, 'There are many who fall and
who rise up to an attitude of rectitude, but there are some
who fall from good deeds to polluted things. Better is he who
falls and rises up than he who stands and then falls.'

He also said, 'I prefer a man who has sinned, and done

wickedly, and repented, to the man who has not sinned and has not manifested repentance; for the former possesses a humble mind, and the latter esteemes himself in his thoughts a just man'[c].

Certain brothers went up to an old man and, making apologies to him, they said, 'Father, what shall we do, for Satan is hunting after us?' And he said to them, 'It is right for you to be watchful and to weep continually. My own thoughts are always fixed upon the place where our Lord was crucified, and I sigh and lament and weep about it always.' And thus having received a good example of repentance the brothers departed and became chosen vessels.

And when Abba Poimen heard that he was dead, that is to say, that Abba Arsenios had gone to his rest, he said, 'Blessed are you, O Abba Arsenios, for you did weep over yourself in this world. For he who weeps not for himself in this world must weep forever in the next. He may weep here voluntarily, or there because of the punishments [which he will receive], but it is impossible for a man to escape weeping either here or there.'

A brother asked Abba Sisoes, saying, 'What shall I do, father? For I have fallen.' The old man said unto him, 'Rise up.' And the brother said to him, 'I did rise up, but I fell again.' The old man said to him, 'Rise up again.' And the brother said to him, 'I did rise up again, many times, and I fell [again].' The old man said to him, 'Rise up again.' And the brother said to him, 'Until when?' The old man said to him, 'Until you advance, either in good deeds or in falling; for in the road wherein a man advances he goes, whether it be to death or to life.'

NILOS THE ASCETIC[13]

The Significance of the Cross

In the biblical story Elisha then threw a stick in the Jordan

38 *Repentance*

and brought to the surface the axe-head his disciple had lost
[cf. 2 Kings 6.6]; that is to say, he revealed a thought which
his disciple believed to be hidden deep within him and he
exposed it to the view of those present. Here the Jordan signifies speaking about repentance, for it was in the Jordan
that John performed the baptism of repentance. Now if
someone does not speak accurately about repentance, but
makes his listeners despise it by failing to communicate its
hidden power, he lets the axe-head fall into the Jordan. But
then a stick — and this signifies the Cross — brings the axe-
head up from the depths to the surface. For prior to the Cross
the full meaning of repentance was hidden and anyone who
tried to say something about it could easily be convicted of
speaking rashly and inadequately. After the Crucifixion,
however, the meaning of repentance became clear to all,
for it had been revealed at the appointed time through the
wood of the Cross.

MARK THE ASCETIC[14]

The 'Primacy' of Repentance

There is a sin which is always 'unto death' [John 5.16]:
the sin for which we do not repent. For this sin even a saint's
prayers will not be heard.

He who repents rightly does not imagine that it is his
own effort which cancels his former sins; but through his
effort he makes peace with God.

No one is as good and as loving as God; but not even
He forgives him who does not repent.

He who has come to the knowledge of truth confesses
to God not as a result of remembering what he has done
but in order to gain patience for what is to come.

Our Lord Jesus Christ defined as one the fitting purposes
for all people, namely repentance . . . All the variety of His
commandments are summed up in the single principle of
repentance.

Repentance, I think, is not restricted to certain times or matters. For old and young alike, repentance remains incomplete until the moment of death . . . We are not, however, condemned for our sins, but for the refusal to repent.

I, therefore, believe that the work of repentance consists of the threads of these three commandments, namely the purification of thoughts, incessant prayer, and endurance of sufferings.

BARSANUPHIOS AND JOHN[15]

The Love of God and the Response of Man

We have a merciful God who knows our weakness more so than we do.

The sign of forgiveness of sins is that one hates them and no longer does them; if, however, one still ponders on them and his heart consents to them, or if he still does them, this is a sign that they have not as yet been forgiven and that he is possessed [or guilty] of them.

You will please God more with your repentance than with your virginity.

DIADOCHOS OF PHOTIKE[16]

A Sacrament of Healing

Just as bodily wounds that are not cared for are hardened and do not feel the bitterness of the medicine used by doctors, yet when they are cleansed they begin to feel the effect of the medicine and consequently are healed rapidly, so also with the soul . . . when it begins to be purified with great care, then it feels the fear of God burning it like a life-giving medicine and it is judged while its passions are burned.

JOHN MOSCHOS[17]

Now Is the Time to Repent

God has granted us this time for repentance, and we must search for it with zeal.

Woe, how much we shall weep and feel remorse over what we do not repent now.

Every age needs to repent, whether young or old.

ISAIAS OF SKETIS[18]

Unceasing Regeneration

If a man performs great signs and miracles, possesses all knowledge and raises the dead, yet he cannot cease caring since he can fall into sin; for he is always in the condition of repentance.

God saw that man was weak and gave him repentance while he is still in the body, until his last breath.

Let us take good care to remain in the protection of repentance, and let us receive nourishment from her holy breasts so that she will nourish us.

JOHN OF KARPATHOS[19]

If You Fall, Arise

Do all in your power not to fall, for the strong athlete should not fall. But if you do fall, get up again at once and continue the contest. Even if you fall a thousand times because of the withdrawal of God's grace, rise up again each time, and keep on doing this until the day of your death. For it is written, 'If a righteous man falls down seven times' — that is, repeatedly throughout his life — 'seven times shall he rise again' [Proverbs 24.16].

HESYCHIOS THE PRIEST[20]

Dependence on God Rather Than on Oneself

Each hour of the day we should note and weigh our actions, and in the evening we should do what we can to free ourselves from the burden of them by means of repentance – if, that is, we wish, with Christ's help, to overcome wickedness. We should also make sure that we perform all our outward tasks in a manner that accords with God's will, before God and for God alone, so that we are not mindlessly seduced by the senses.

We will travel the road of repentance correctly if, as we begin to give attention to the intellect, we combine humility with watchfulness, and prayer with the power to rebut evil thoughts. In this way we will adorn the chamber of our hearts with the holy and venerable name of Jesus Christ as with a lighted lamp, and will sweep our hearts clean of wickedness, purifying and embellishing them. But if we trust only in our own watchfulness and attentiveness, we shall quickly be pushed aside by our enemies. We shall be overturned and cast down by their extreme craftiness. We will become ever more fully entangled in their nets of evil thought, and will readily be slaughtered by them, lacking as we do the powerful sword of the name of Jesus Christ. For only this sword, swiftly turning in the undivided heart, is able to cut them down, to burn and obliterate them as fire the reed.

THEOGNOSTOS AND THEODOROS[21]

The Wrath and Compassion of God

We will not be punished or condemned in the age to be because we have sinned, since we were given a mutable and unstable nature. But we will be punished if, after sinning, we do not repent and turn from our evil ways to the Lord; for we have been given the power to repent, as well as the time in which to do so. Only through repentance shall we receive God's mercy, and not its opposite, His passionate anger. Not that God is angry with us: He is angry with evil. Indeed, the divine is beyond passion and vengefulness, though we speak of it as reflecting, like a mirror, our actions and dispositions, giving to each of us whatever we deserve.

ELIAS THE PRESBYTER[22]

Refusal to Repent

Those who deliberately refuse to repent sin continually; those who sin without meaning to not only repent with all their heart, but also do not often have cause to repent.

PETER OF DAMASCUS[23]

The Gift from Above

If we so wish, however, God's second gift of grace — repentance — can lead us back to our former beauty. But if we fail to repent, inevitably we will depart with the unrepentant demons into age-long punishment, more by our own free choice than against our will. Yet God did not create us for wrath but for salvation [cf. 1 Thessalonians 5.9], so that we might enjoy His blessings; and we should therefore be thankful and grateful towards our Benefactor. But our failure to get to know His gifts has made us indolent, and indolence has made us forgetful, with the result that ignorance rules over us.

It is less difficult to cleanse an impure soul than to restore to health a soul which was once cleansed but has been wounded anew. For it is less difficult for those who have recently renounced the confusion of the world to attain dispassion, whatever faults they may previously have committed, than it is for those who have tasted the blessed words of God and walked in the path of salvation and then gone

back to sin. This is due partly to the influence of bad habit
and partly to the fact that the demon of dejection is always
dangling the image of sin before them. But, with the coopera-
tion of divine grace, a diligent and assiduous soul may readily achieve even this difficult feat of regaining its dispassion; for, long-suffering and compassionate, grace invites us
to repentance, and with inexpressible mercy accepts those
who return, as we have been taught in the Gospels through
the parable of the prodigal son [cf. Luke 15.11-32].

That One Should Not Despair

Even if you are not what you should be, you should not
despair. It is bad enough that you have sinned; why in ad-
dition do you wrong God by regarding Him in your ignorance as powerless? Is He, who for your sake created the
great universe that you behold, incapable of saving your
soul? And if you say that this fact, as well as His incarnation, only makes your condemnation worse, then repent;
and He will receive your repentance, as He accepted that
of the prodigal son [cf. Luke 15.20] and the prostitute [cf.
Luke 7.37-50]. But if repentance is too much for you, and
you sin out of habit even when you do not want to, show
humility like the publican [cf. Luke 18.13]: this is enough
to ensure your salvation. For he who sins without repenting, yet does not despair, must of necessity regard himself
as the lowest of creatures, and will not dare to judge or cen-
sure anyone. Rather, he will marvel at God's compassion,
and will be full of gratitude towards his Benefactor, and so
may receive many other blessings as well. Even if he is subject to the devil in that he sins, yet from fear of God he
disobeys the enemy when the latter tries to make him despair. Because of this he has his portion with God; for he
is grateful, gives thanks, is patient, fears God, does not judge
so that he may not be judged. All these are crucial quali-
ties. It is as Saint John Chrysostom says about Gehenna:
it is almost of greater benefit to us than the kingdom of
heaven, since because of it many may enter the kingdom

of heaven, while few enter for the sake of the kingdom itself; and if they do enter it, it is by virtue of God's compassion. Gehenna pursues us with fear, the kingdom embraces
us with love, and through them both we are saved by God's
grace.

The Benefit of Genuine Repentance

It is always possible to make a new start by means of
repentance. 'You fell,' it is written, 'now arise' [cf. Proverbs
24.16]. And if you fall again, then rise again, without despairing at all of your salvation, no matter what happens. So long
as you do not surrender yourself willingly to the enemy, your
patient endurance, combined with self-reproach, will suffice
for your salvation. 'For at one time we ourselves went astray
in our folly and disobedience,' says Saint Paul '. . . Yet He
saved us, not because of any good things we had done, but
in His mercy' [Titus 3.3,5]. So do not despair in any way,
ignoring God's help, for He can do whatever He wishes. On
the contrary, place your hope in Him and He will do one
of these things: either through trials and temptations, or in
some other way which He alone knows, He will bring about
your restoration; or He will accept your patient endurance
and humility in the place of works; or because of your hope
He will act lovingly towards you in some other way of which
you are not aware, and so will save your shackled soul. Only
do not abandon your Physician, for otherwise you will suffer senselessly the twofold death because you do not know
the hidden ways of God.

Fear of God

Fear brings about repentance, says Saint Isaak, and
through repentance comes the revelation of hidden things.
This is how we should meditate on the fear of God. After the
service of Compline each of us should recite the Creed and
the Lord's Prayer, and then repeat 'Lord, have mercy' many
times. We should sit facing east, like someone mourning

for the dead, moving our heads backward and forward with
pain in our souls and with a grieving heart, and saying the
words appropriate to our particular stage of knowledge,
beginning with the first stage, until we attain the state of
prayer. Then we should fall upon our faces before God with
inexpressible joy and should begin to pray. First our prayer
should be thanksgiving, then confession of our sins, and then
the other words of prayer . . . Saint Athanasios the Great
says that we should confess the sins we have committed in
ignorance, as well as those that we would have committed
had we not been saved from them by God's grace, so that
these may not be counted against us in the hour of our death.
We should also pray for each other, according to the commandment of the Lord [cf. Luke 22.32] and of the Apostle
James [cf. James 5.16].

Repenting Is Not Making Excuses

For repentance, properly speaking, is the eradication of
evil, says Saint John Chrysostom; while what are called acts
of repentance or prostrations are a bending of the knees,
which expresses that a person who bows sincerely before
God and man after having offended someone assumes the
attitude of a servant. By doing this he can claim in self-
defense that he has not answered back at all or attempted
to justify himself, as did the Pharisee, but is more like the
publican in considering himself the least of all men and unworthy to lift his eyes to heaven [cf. Luke 18.11-13]. For if
he thinks he is repentant and nevertheless tries to refute
the person who – rightly or wrongly – is judging him, he
is not worthy of the grace of forgiveness, since he acts as
if he seeks a hearing in court and the opportunity to justify
himself, hoping to achieve what he wants through a due pro-
cess of law. Such behavior is entirely at variance with the
Lord's commandments. And naturally so; for if one attempts
to justify himself, then one is appealing to lawful rights, not
to love for one's fellowmen. In such a case grace is no longer
our guiding principle – the grace that justifies the ungodly

without the works of righteousness [cf. Romans 4.5], but
only on condition that we are grateful for rebukes and endure them with forbearance, giving thanks to those who rebuke us and remaining patient and unresentful before our
accusers. In this way our prayer will be pure and our repentance effective. For the more we pray for those who slander
and accuse us, the more God pacifies those who bear enmity towards us and also gives us peace through our pure
and persistent prayer.

The Boundless Mercy of God Is Loving and Consuming

In this way he emulates the psalmist, who wrote: 'Lord,
my heart is not haughty, nor are my eyes presumptuous'
[Psalms 131.1]. But after reaching such heights he must be
careful lest through negligence or self-inflation he suffer
what David suffered, without perhaps being able to repent
as David did. For to sin, even in the case of those who are
most righteous, is easy, while repentance is not easy for
everyone because death is near; and even before death
comes there is despair. It is good, then, not to fall; or, if we
fall, to rise again. And should we fall, we should not despair
and so estrange ourselves from the Lord's love. For if He
so chooses, He can deal mercifully with our weakness. Only
we should not cut ourselves off from Him or feel oppressed
when constrained by His commandments, nor should we
lose heart when we fall short of our goal. Rather, let us learn
that a thousand years in the sight of the Lord are but a single
day, and a single day is a thousand years [cf. Psalms 90.4].
Let us neither be hasty nor tardy, and let us always be ready
to make a new start. If you fall, rise up. If you fall again,
rise up again. Only do not abandon your Physician, lest you
be condemned as worse than a suicide because of your despair. Wait on Him, and he will be merciful, either reform-
ing you, or sending you trials, or through some other provi-
sion of which you are ignorant.

Being bountiful and full of love, God awaits with great
patience the repentance of every sinner, and He celebrates

the return of the sinner with celestial rejoicing; as He Himself says, 'There is joy in heaven over one sinner who repents' [cf. Luke 15.7,10]. But when someone sees this generosity and patience, and how God awaits repentance and so does not punish sins one by one, he may neglect the commandment and make such generosity an excuse for indifference, adding sin to sin, offense to offense, laziness to laziness. In this way he will reach the furthest limits of sin, and fall into such transgression that he is not able to recover himself. On the contrary, sinking into the lowest depths and finally committing himself to the devil, he destroys himself. This is what happened to the people of Sodom: reaching and even going beyond the furthest limits of sin − for not a single spark of repentance was to be found among them − they were consumed by the fire of divine justice [cf. Genesis 19.1-28]. It also happened in the time of Noah: people had surrendered so unrestrainedly to the impulses of evil, piling up such a load of sin on themselves and showing not the least sign of repentance, that the whole earth became corrupt [cf. Genesis 6.5]. Similarly, God was bountiful to the Egyptians, although they had sinned greatly and had maltreated His people: He did not hand them over to total destruction, but through gradual chastisement He induced them to repent. Yet when they lapsed and returned enthusiastically to their evil ways and their original disbelief, finally even pursuing the Lord's people as they departed from Egypt, divine justice destroyed them completely [cf. Exodus 14.23-28]. God also showed His habitual forbearance towards the people of Israel, although they too had sinned greatly and had killed His prophets. Yet when they became so committed to evil that they did not respect even the royal dignity of His Son, but laid murderous hands upon Him, they were utterly rejected and cast aside: prophecy, priesthood and service were taken from them and were entrusted to the Gentiles who believed [cf. Matthew 21.33-43].

Surrender to Christ

Let us draw near eagerly to Christ who summons us,

surrendering our hearts to Him, and let us not despair of
our salvation, deliberately giving ourselves over to evil. For
it is a trick of the devil to lead us to despair by reminding
us of our past sins. We must realize that if Christ, when on
earth, healed and restored the blind, the paralyzed and the
dumb, and raised the dead that were already in a state of
decomposition, how much more will He heal blindness of
mind, paralysis of soul, and dumbness of the dissolute heart.
For He who created the body also created the soul. And if
He was so bounteous and merciful to what is mortal and
disintegrates, how much more compassionate and healing
will He be to the immortal soul, overpowered by the sickness of evil and ignorance, when it turns to Him and asks
Him for help? For it is He who said: 'Will not My heavenly
Father vindicate those who call to Him night and day? Yes,
I assure you, He will vindicate them swiftly' [cf. Luke 18.7-8];
and: 'Ask and it will be given to you, seek and you will find,
knock and it will be opened to you' [Matthew 7.7]; and again:
'If he will not give to him out of friendship, yet on account
of his persistence he will get up and give him what he needs'
[cf. Luke 11.8]. Moreover, He came so that sinners should
turn back to Him [cf. Matthew 9.13]. Only let us devote
ourselves to the Lord, rejecting insofar as we can our evil
prepossessions, and He will not overlook us, but will be
ready to offer us His help.

KALLISTOS AND IGNATIOS[24]

The Door of Mercy

Let us not be sorrowful when we fall into some sin, but
only when we persist in that state. For a fall often occurs
even to the perfect, but persistence in sin is perfect mor-
tification. . . . We must realize that at all times, in fact during the entire twenty-four hours of the day and night, we
need to repent. . . . Repentance is grace upon grace granted
to man; it is a second regeneration from God and, just as

we have received the pledge of faith, through repentance we receive His grace. Repentance is the door of mercy opened to those who pursue it . . . It is the second grace, born in the heart as a result of faith and fear.

BENEDICT OF NURSIA[49]

Anticipated Judgement

Every day with tears and sighs confess your past sins to God in prayer and change from these evil ways in the future. And finally, never lose hope in God's mercy. Whether he sits, walks or stands, one's head must be bowed and his eyes cast down. Judging himself always guilty on account of his sins, he should consider that he is already at the fearful judgement, and constantly say in his heart what the publican in the Gospel said with downcast eyes: 'Lord, I am a sinner, not worthy to look up at heaven' [Luke 18.13]. And with the Prophet: 'I am bowed down and humbled in every way' [Psalms 37.7-9, 118.107].

GREGORY THE GREAT[26]

The Interdependence of Contrition and Humility

On the other hand, those who desist from sinning but do not lament their sins are to be admonished not to suppose that their sins are forgiven on the mere plea that they have not been repeated, if they have not been cleansed by tears. A writer, for instance, who has given up writing, has not deleted what he has written just because he has not added anything. So, too, one does not make reparation for insults offered merely by holding one's peace, for in truth it is necessary that he abjure the words of his former pride by expressions of subsequent humility. Nor again is a debtor discharged merely because he incurs no further debts, if he has not paid the debts already incurred. So, too, when we we sin against God, we certainly do not make reparation merely by ceasing from evil, unless those sinful pleasures we have indulged in are succeeded by sorrow abjuring them. Indeed, even if no sin of deed had stained us in this life, our innocence would not by any means suffice to save us so long as we live here, for there would still be much that is unlawful to knock at our hearts. With what assurance, then, does he feel secure who, having committed evil, is a witness against himself that he is not innocent?

It is not that God is regaled by our tortures; no, He heals the diseases of our sins by their contrary antidotes, so that we who have departed from Him by the delight of pleasures may return to him in tearful grief and, having fallen by losing ourselves amid sinful things, we may rise up by restraining ourselves even in what is lawful. The heart which has been flooded with insane delight He wants made clean by a saving sorrow, and wounds inflicted by the elation of pride He wants healed by the lowliness of a humble life. Wherefore, Scripture says: 'I said to the wicked, do not act wickedly, and to the sinners, lift not up the horn.' Sinners lift up the horn if they fail to acknowledge their wickedness and to do humble penance. Wherefore, it is said again: 'A contrite and humbled heart God does not despise.' For anyone who bewails his sins, but does not desist from them, has a contrite heart, indeed, but scorns to humble it; whereas he who desists from sin, but does not bewail it, does, indeed, humble himself, but fails to have a contrite heart.

ISAAK THE SYRIAN[27]

The Need for Hope

Although one falls, he does not forget the love of his Father; and although he is loaded with trespasses of every kind, his zeal for the service of good is not held back, nor does he desist from his course, nor abhor to stand in struggle against these things anew and with the same chance of being vanquished, nor cease from demolishing every day his building and beginning a [new] foundation.

And the word of the Prophet is in his mouth: 'Till the hour of my departure from this world, rejoice not against me, O mine enemy: when I fall, I shall arise; when I sit in darkness, the Lord shall be a light unto me.' And he will not cease to struggle until his death.

The Gate Opened through Tears

Then he is deemed worthy of the gift of tears, flowing abundantly and without compulsion. Tears are to the mind the sure distinction between the bodily and the spiritual state, between the state of apperception and that of purity. When he begins to leave the bodiliness of this world and moves in that territory which lies beyond this visible nature, then at once he will reach the grace of tears. And from the first apartment of that hidden behavior these tears will begin and they will conduct him to the complete love of God. When he has reached this point, tears will be so copious that he drinks them with his food and his drink, so constant and abundant are they. This is a true token of the mind's leaving this world and its apperceiving the spiritual world. And the more the mind approaches unto this world, the more these tears will diminish. And when the mind is wholly in worldly things, it will be completely without tears, and this is a sign of its being enveloped by the affections.

For if anyone weeps constantly, the affections will not approach his heart; for weeping lies beyond affectability. If tears are able to efface from the mind of him that mourns and weeps, for but a short time, the recollection of the affections, what shall we say about him who has imposed upon himself a definite service during the day and night? Who knows the profits of weeping, save those who have given themselves to it? All the Saints desire this [means of] introduction; and by weeping a gate is opened before them through which they enter that place of consolation, in which the footsteps of God's love are impressed by revelations.

The Boundless Love of God Compels All

Repentance is fitting at all times and for all persons, to sinners as well as to the righteous who look for salvation. There are no bounds to perfection, for even the perfection of the most perfect is naught but imperfection. Hence, until the moment of death neither the time nor the works of repentance can ever be complete.

O the power of His almightiness! O His immeasurable kindness toward our nature, that He also brings sinners into existence! The retribution of the sinners is this, that He repays them with resurrection instead of with justice.

Thus he that is entangled in evil things has not to be dejected, for it is possible for him to gain life, as he is still alive. There is hope for him as well as for the one who behaves well. Why do you rebuke the sinner, O man? The labors of your own merchandise have not yet entered the harbor; the hope of him over whom you are extolling yourself has not been cut off by God. It is possible that in a short time he will surpass you in excellence and come nearer to God than you are. For death has not yet come and concluded his affair, nor yours. Many vicissitudes happen to a man during his life. But it is God who looks to the end and not to the things in the middle. There have been many righteous men who fell from their righteousness, and sinners have come up and taken their place. Therefore the righteous man should not extol himself, he is still alive; nor shall the sinner be dejected, for God is near to him if he seeks Him, and prepared to receive him when he changes his behavior and turns toward Him. If you have wrought righteousness without perceiving the taste of its profit, be not amazed.

Repentance As Regeneration

Repentance is the mother of life. It opens to us its gate when we flee from all things. The grace which we have lost, after baptism, by lax behavior, is restored in us by repentance, through discrimination of mind. From water and spirit

we have put on Christ, without perceiving His glory. By
repentance we enter into His delight through the dis-
criminating love which rises in us.

He who is destitute of repentance is destitute of future
delight. He who is near to all is far from repentance. He who
is far from all, with discrimination, is the true repentant.
As soon as a man withdraws from men and concentrates
upon himself, impulses of repentance will show themselves
in his mind. He receives the seed of life from grace and,
as an embryo, the affection of discrimination moves in him,
and in his heart is stirred the thought of eternal life in the
future and the hope of resurrection and the thought of
judgement.

Do not think that without divine grace suffering falls into
the mind, which receives [it] secretly, as a gift through divine
mercy, because of a sudden contrition and a longing after
life. As the blessed Evagrios says: 'A purifying drug is the
hot contrition of the soul, which is given by the Lord through
the angels to those who repent, that through diligence purification from the affections may be granted.' Further he says:
'The fire of a furnace is the hot contrition of the soul, which
through the grace of Christ happens to the soul at the time
of prayer so that the thoughts attain contemplation. Its lack
is cured by living water.'

The beginning of repentance is humbleness without ar-
tifice. Splendid garments are a confusion of repentance. The
way towards wisdom is the regulation of the limbs. Bodily
effervescences are a confusion of wisdom. True wisdom is
looking towards God. Looking towards God is silence of the
deliberations. Solitude of the mind is quietness with discrimination. The moisture of the senses is a fountain of deliberations. Apperception in God is the depth of humbleness.

Repentance and Tears

Many show the appearance of repentance; but only he
possesses it in truth who is grieved in heart. Many run to

find the affection of the heart; but only he finds it in truth
who possesses continual silence. Everyone who is a servant
of God loves grief.

Repentance is the constant sorrow of the heart at the
meditation of that inexplicable statute: how shall I reach that
unspeakable entrance? If you love repentance, then love also
solitude. For without this repentance cannot be completed.
If there is anyone who disputes this, do not dispute with
him, for he does not know what he says. If he knew what
repentance was, he also would know its place, and that it
is not to be disturbed by trouble. If you love solitude, the
father of repentance, then love also to accept gladly the small
deficiencies of the body, and the blame that arises from
them. Without this preparation it will be impossible for you
to live in solitude, freely, without trouble. If you despise
those things, you will acquire solitude, according to God's
will. If you are wronged or robbed or laughed at or the like,
you will not be moved, because of your love of solitude.

Metanoia and Prayer

Therefore God demands the alteration of the mind. By
the mind we acquire improvement and by the mind we become despicable. So this alone is sufficient, without [any
further] help, to stand before God and to speak in our behalf.

The explanation of the denotation of repentance, in its
real practical sense, is continual mournful supplication in
contrite prayer, offered to God for the forgiveness of pre-
vious sins, and petition to be guarded against future ones.
Therefore our Lord also has sustained our weakness by
prayer: 'Watch and pray, that you enter not into temptation'
[Matthew 26.41]. And: 'Pray, and do not faint' [Luke 18.1].

It is said concerning one of our Fathers that for forty years
his prayer consisted of one sentence: 'I have sinned as man;
but You as God forgive me.' And the fathers and brethren
heard him repeating this sentence, weeping passionately,
without ceasing. And this prayer alone, during night and day

took for him the place of service.

MAXIMOS THE CONFESSOR[28]

For these five reasons will the soul abstain from sin: the fear of men, the fear of judgement, the future reward, the love of God, or finally, the prompting of conscience.

JOHN KLIMAKOS[29]

Step Five – 'On Penitence'

Repentance is the renewal of baptism and is a contract with God for a fresh start in life. Repentance goes shopping for humility and is ever distrustful of bodily comfort. Repentance is critical awareness and a sure watch over oneself. Repentance is the daughter of hope and the refusal of despair. (The penitent stands guilty – but undisgraced.) Repentance is reconciliation with the Lord by performance of good deeds which are the opposite of sin. It is the purification of conscience and the voluntary endurace of affliction. The penitent deals out his own punishment, for repentance is the fierce persecution of the stomach and the flogging of the soul into intense awareness . . .

The words of David could surely be seen to be fulfilled [in the Prison], for there were men in hardship and bowed down to the end of their lives, going about each day in sadness, their bodies' wounds stinking of rottenness [Psalms 37.6-7] and yet unnoticed by them. They forgot to eat their bread; their drink was mixed with tears. They ate dust and ashes instead of bread; their bones stuck to their flesh and they were dried up like grass [Psalms 101.4-12]. The only words you could hear from them were these: 'Woe, woe, alas! It is just, it is just. Spare us, spare us, O Lord!' Some said, 'Be merciful, be merciful'; others, more sadly, 'Forgive us, Lord, forgive us, if it is possible.'

An old habit often dominates even someone who mourns. No wonder, for the judgements visited by God and our own lapses make up a list hard to understand, and it is impossible to be sure which of our failings are due to carelessness, which are due to the fact that God permitted them, and which arise from God's having turned away from us. I have been told, however, that lapses occurring as a result of divine providence cause us to repent swiftly, since He who delivers us does not permit us to be held captive for long. But above all we must fight off the demon of dejection whenever we happen to slip, for he comes right beside us when we are praying and reminds us of our former good standing with God and tries to divert us from our prayer.

Do not be surprised if you fall every day and do not surrender. Stand your ground bravely, and you may be sure that your guardian angel will respect your endurance. A fresh, warm wound is easier to heal than those that are old, neglected, festering, and in need of extensive treatment, surgery, bandaging, and cauterization. Long neglect can render many of them incurable. However, all things are possible with God [Matthew 19.26].

God is merciful before a fall, inexorable after − so the demons say. And when you have sinned, pay no attention to him who says in regard to minor failings: 'If only you had not committed that major fault! This is nothing by comparison.' The truth is that very often small gifts soften the great anger of the Judge.

He who really keeps track of what he has done will consider as lost every day during which he did not mourn, regardless of whatever good he may happen to have done.

Let no one who grieves for his sins expect reassurance at the hour of death, There can be no assurance about the unknown. 'Spare me before I depart from here, unsure of my salvation' [Psalms 38.14].

Where the Spirit of the Lord is, there the chains of sin are let loose; where there is real humility, all bonds are made free; but those without the one or the other should not be deceived: they are in bondage. Those living in the world are [very often] without these two assurances, especially the first, unless, through almsgiving, some so run their race that they know at the moment of death how much they have gained.

He who weeps for himself will not be wrapped up in the grief, lapse, or reproach of someone else. A dog injured by a wild animal becomes all the more maddened against it and is driven to implacable rage by the pain of the injury.

We ought to be on our guard, in case our conscience has stopped troubling us, not so much because of its being clear as because of its being immersed in sin.

A proof of our having been delivered from our failings is the unceasing acknowledgement of our indebtedness.

Nothing equals the mercy of God or surpasses it. To despair is therefore to inflict death on oneself.

A sign of true repentance is the admission that all our troubles, and more besides, whether visible or not, are richly deserved.

After Moses had seen God in the bush, he went back to Egypt, that is, to the darkness and the brick-making of Pharaoh, who is to be understood here in the spiritual sense. But he returned to the bush; and not only to the bush, but to the mountaintop. For anyone who has experienced contemplation will never despair of himself. The great Job became a beggar, but afterwards he became twice as rich.

If you have no courage, if you are lazy, then lapses that occur (after entering religious life) are hard to bear. They wipe out the hope of dispassion and they make us imagine that true blessedness is simply to rise from the pit of sin. But note well that we never return by the road on which we strayed, but rather by a different and shorter route.

I saw two men travelling the same route to the Lord, and at the same time. One of them was older, and had worked harder. The other, his disciple, soon overtook him and was first to arrive at the sepulchre of humility.

All of us, but especially the lapsed, should be particularly careful not to be afflicted with the disease that . . . uses God's love for man as an excuse and is very welcome to those who are lovers of pleasure.

In my meditation or, more accurately, in my acts of repentance, a fire of prayer will burn and will consume everything material. Let the holy prisoners, described above, be a rule for you, a pattern, a model, a true picture of repentance, so that for as long as you live you will have no need of a treatise; until at last Christ, the divine Son of God, will enlighten you in the resurrection of true repentance.

SYMEON THE NEW THEOLOGIAN[30]

Repentance Must Be Constant and with Tears

Hour by hour, day by day, let us renew ourselves through repentance in order to learn how to fight and wrestle with the demons who constantly war against us.

Repentance is the door that leads from darkness to light. He who does not enter the light has not entered well through the gate of repentance; for had he done so, he would be in the light. He who does not repent sins precisely, does not repent.

The soul that has begun to burn with divine desire first of all sees the darkness of passions rising as smoke in the fire of the Spirit and reflects its blackness, and begins to weep . . . [a]

For this reason, brethren, let penitence be the task of us all that not only accompanies all others but takes precedence over them. With it is joined weeping and the tears that follow it. There is no weeping without repentance, there are no tears apart from weeping; these three things are interconnected so that it is not possible for the one to appear without the other. Let no one say that it is impossible to weep daily! He who says that it is impossible to repent every day subverts all the divine Scriptures, not to mention the very command of the Lord that says, 'Repent, for the kingdom

of heaven is at hand' [Matthew 4.17], and again, 'Ask, and
it will be given you; seek, and you will find; knock, and it
will be opened to you' [Matthew 7.7, Luke 11.9]. For if you
say that it is impossible daily to repent and to weep and shed
tears, then how can you say that it is possible for men who
are subject to corruption ever to attain to a humble mind,
to rejoice at all times and pray without ceasing [1 Thessalonians 5.17], let alone attain to a heart that is pure from all
kinds of passions and evil thoughts so that one may see God
[Matthew 5.8]? You would not, for you would in that case
be demoted to the ranks of unbelievers [cf. Luke 12.46] instead of being with believers. If God has spoken of these
things as being possible for us, if He says that they are and
daily proclaims it, and you flatly contradict Him by claim-
ing that for us they are not feasible but impossible, you are
not at all different from unbelievers. . . .

It is a good thing to repent, and so is the benefit that
comes from it. The Lord Jesus Christ, our God, knowing this
and foreseeing all things, said, 'Repent, for the kingdom of
heaven is at hand' [Matthew 4.17]. Do you want to learn why
it is impossible for us to be saved without repentance, a
heart-felt repentance such as the word [of Scripture] requires
from us? Listen to the Apostle himself as he proclaims: 'Every
other sin which a man commits is outside the body, but the
fornicator sins against his own body' [1 Corinthians 6.18].
Again he says, 'We must appear before the judgement seat
of Christ, so that each one may receive good or evil, according to what he has done in the body' [2 Corinthians 5.10].
One thus has frequent occasion to say: 'I give thanks to God
that I have not defiled a member of my body by any wicked
action.' This I cannot say for myself, for I am a worker of
all lawlessness! So one has comfort from the fact that he is
without any bodily sin. But to such a person the Master re-
plies by telling the parable of the Ten Virgins [Matthew
25.1-13], showing and making clear to us all that there is
no profit in bodily purity unless the other virtues are present as well. Moreover, Saint Paul himself, in agreement with

his Master, proclaims, 'Strive for peace with all men, and for the holiness without which no one will see the Lord' [Hebrews 12.14]. Why did he say 'Strive?' Because it is not possible for us to become holy and to be saints in an hour! We must therefore progress from modest beginnings toward holiness and purity. Even were we to spend a thousand years in this life we should never perfectly attain to it. Rather we must always struggle for it every day, as if mere beginners. This again he himself has shown us by saying: 'Not that I have already obtained this or am already perfect' [Philippians 3.12].

Therefore I entreat you, my brethren, pay attention and listen to the words of a sinner, the least of your brethren. 'Come, let us worship and fall down' [Psalms 95.6] before our holy God who loves mankind. 'Let us come before His presence with thanksgiving' [Psalms 95.2] 'and weep before the Lord our Maker, for He is the Lord our God, and we are His people and the sheep of His pasture' [Psalms 95.6-7], 'that He may not turn away His face from us' [Psalms 102.2]. Let us repent with all our heart and cast away not only our evil deeds, but also the wicked and unclean thoughts of our hearts and obliterate them in accordance with that which is written: 'Rend your hearts and not your garments' [Joel 2.13]. Tell me: Of what use is it if we distribute all our goods to the poor, but fail to make a break with evil and to hate sin? Of what use is it if, while we do not actively commit bodily sin, we mentally engage in shameful and unclean thoughts and invisibly commit sin and are governed and controlled by restrained passions of soul? I beseech you, let us cast away, together with our wealth, the habit of servitude to the evils we have mentioned. Nor let us stop at this, but let us eagerly wash away their defilement with tears of penitence.

Some Examples of Penitence among Laymen

So it is possible for all men, brethren, not only for monks but for laymen as well, to be penitent at all times and

constantly, and to weep and entreat God, and by such practices to acquire all other virtues as well. That this is true
John of golden words [Chrysostom], the great pillar and doc-
tor of the Church, bears witness with me. In his discourse
on David, as he expounds on the Fiftieth Psalm, he asserts
that this is possible for one who has wife and children, men
and women servants, a large household, and great posses-
sions, and who is prominent in worldly affairs. Not only is
he able daily to weep and pray and repent, but he can also
attain to perfection of virtue if he so wishes. He can receive the Holy Spirit and become a friend of God and enjoy
the vision of Him. Such men before Christ's coming were
Abraham, Isaak, Jacob, Lot at Sodom, and (to pass over the
rest who are too many [to enumerate]) Moses and David.
Under the new grace and dispensation of our God and
Savior, Peter, the unlettered fisherman who had a mother-
in law and other [relatives], proclaimed the God who had
been revealed. Who could count those others, more
numerous than the rain drops [Sirach 1.2] and the stars of
heaven [Genesis 15.5], kings, rulers, prominent men, not
to mention poor people and those in moderate circumstances? They have cities and houses and the sanctuaries
of churches, which they have built with liberality; their
homes for the aged and hospices for strangers remain and
exist to this day. All the things they acquired during their
lifetime they used with piety, not as though they owned
them, but rather like servants of the Master who administers
what He has entrusted to them according to His pleasure
and who will, as Paul says, 'deal with the world as though
they had no dealings with it' [1 Corinthians 7.31]. For this
reason they have become glorious and illustrious even in
this present life, and now and to endless ages they will
become even more glorious and illustrious in the kingdom
of God. If instead of being timid, slothful, and despisers of
God's commandments, we were zealous, watchful, and
sober, we should have no need of renunciation or tonsure
or flight from the world.

Seeking the Light with Tears

But to you who are Christ's servants, who are anxious
to learn and have prepared your ears to hear, the Master
of all things shouts through His holy Gospels, saying, 'While
you have the light, run to the light, lest the darkness over-
take you [cf. John 12.35-36]. By repentance run in the way
of His commandments [cf. Psalms 19.32]. Run, run, while
it is still the time when He shines on you, before the night
of death overtakes you [cf. John 9.4] and you are sent away
into eternal darkness. Run, seek, knock, that the door of the
kingdom of heaven may be opened unto you [cf. Matthew
7.7, Luke 11.9] and you may enter within it and have it
within you [cf. Luke 17.21]. As for those who depart from
this present life without attaining to it, how will they ever
find it once they have gone there? Accordingly, it is here
that we have been commanded to ask, to seek, and to knock
by means of penitence and tears, and the Master has promised to give it to us if we do so. If then we refuse to do this
and to obey Christ our Master, so that we may endeavor
to receive the kingdom within ourselves while we are still
in this life, we will not deserve to hear Him speak to us when
we have departed thither and say, 'Why are you now seeking the kingdom which you refused when I was giving it
to you? Were you not unwilling when I earnestly entreated
you to exert yourselves to receive it from Me? Have you not
despised it and preferred to enjoy corruptible and earthly
things? By what deeds or words will you be able to find it
from now on?'

Therefore, fathers and brethren, I exhort you, let us keep
God's commandments with all eagerness, in order that we
may obtain the eternal life and kingdom. May we never hear
in this life [these words addressed to us], 'He who does not
obey the Son shall not see life, but the wrath of God rests
upon him' [John 3.36], nor in the world to come, 'Depart from
Me' [Matthew 7.23], 'I do not know where you come from'
[Luke 13.25]. Rather may we listen to that blessed voice as
it says 'Come, O blessed of My Father, inherit the kingdom

prepared for you, because you fed Me when I was hungry for your salvation by practicing My commandments, you gave Me drink, you clothed Me, you welcomed Me, you visited Me [cf. Matthew 25.43ff] by cleansing your hearts from every spot and defilement of sin. Now enjoy My blessings whose enjoyment is ineffable, and is eternal and immortal life.' May we all obtain this, through the grace of our Lord Jesus Christ, to whom be glory forever.

But those who have not yet experienced this or been found worthy thereof are all subject to the Law, which was prior to grace. They are slaves [cf. Galatians 4.7] and disciples of slaves, hearers of the Law [cf. Romans 2.13], children of the slave-woman [Galatians 4.31] and sons of darkness [cf. 1 Thessalonians 5.5], even though they may be emperors and patriarchs, prelates or priests, whether rulers or subjects, lay persons or monks, ascetics or superiors, poor or rich, physically ill or in good health. All who sit in darkness [cf. Luke 1.79] are sons of darkness and are unwilling to repent. For penitence is the gateway that leads out of darkness into light. He who does not enter into the light [cf. John 3.20] has not properly gone through the gate of repentance; for, had he done so, he would have been in the light. He who does not repent commits sin, because he is not penitent, for 'whoever knows what is right to do and fails to do it, for him it is sin' [James 4.17]. He 'who commits sin is the slave of sin' [John 8.34] and 'hates the light and does not come to the light, lest his deeds should be exposed' [John 3.20]. But now we have willingly and of our own accord entered into the light through penitence and are convicted and judged [cf. Ephesians 5.13], but this happens mystically and in secret in the innermost chamber of our souls. We undergo this for our purification and for the forgiveness of our offenses by the mercy and love of God towards men, as God alone, as well as we ourselves, understands our condition. On the other hand, when the Lord comes to those who now hate the light and are unwilling to come to it [John 3.20], the light that now is hidden will be revealed and all that they have hidden will become manifest. Whatever each of us men is now, as we wrap ourselves up and refuse to reveal our condition by penitence, the light will then make it clear and manifest to God and to all men.[b]

The Incarnation As Our Possiblility To Be Freed from Sin

And so let no one invent excuses for his sins and say that we, by virtue of the transgression of Adam, are entirely subject to the action of the devil and are dragged by force into sin. They who think and speak thus consider that the dispensation of the Incarnation of our Master and Savior Jesus Christ was useless and vain. Such an opinion is the opinion of heretics and not of the Orthodox. For what other reason did Christ descend and become incarnate, and for what else did He suffer if not in order to loose the condemnation which proceeded from sin, and to deliver our race from slavery to the devil and from the activity in us of this our enemy? This is true autonomy: in no way to be subject to someone else. We are all born sinners from our forefather Adam who sinned; we are all criminals from a criminal, slaves of sin from a slave of sin, subject to the curse and death from him who was subject to the curse and death. And because of Adam who received the action of the cunning devil, and by his counsel was moved to sin, and enslaved himself to him and lost his autonomy, we also, as his children, are subject to the action and the compulsory dominion of the devil and are his slaves. But our Lord came down from the heavens, was incarnate and became man like us in everything except sin, in order to annihilate sin. He was conceived and born so as to sanctify the conception and birth of men. He was raised up and grew little by little so as to bless every age of life. He began to preach at the age of thirty, having become a full-grown Man, so as to teach us not to jump out of line and go before those who are greater than us in mind and virtue, that is, are more intelligent and virtuous than we, especially if we are still young and not perfect in

understanding and virtue. He preserved all the commandments of His God and Father so as to loose every transgression and to deliver us criminals from condemnation. He became a slave, took the form of a slave, in order to raise us,
the slaves of the devil, once more into the condition of masters and to make us masters and possessors over the devil
himself, our former tyrant. (This is confirmed by the saints
who have cast out the devil, as a weak and infirm one, as
well as his servants, not only in their lifetime but also after
their death.) He was hung upon a cross and became a curse,
as the prophet says, 'Cursed is everyone that hangs upon
a tree' [Deuteronomy 21.23], in order to loose the whole
curse of Adam. He died in order to put death to death, and
He rose in order to annihilate the power and activity of the
devil who had authority over us by means of death and
sin.[c]

NIKOLAS KABASILAS[31]

How Love of Christ Leads to True Repentance

Having made this effort and used these opportunities for
considering the matter we may arrive at a knowledge of the
dignity of our nature, and also a clear perception of the
loving-kindness of God. Indeed, this will prevent us from
even looking at anything evil, and should we happen to fall
it will readily raise us up again.

Of the many things which impede our salvation, the
greatest of all is that when we commit any transgression and
we do not at once turn back to God and ask forgiveness.
Because we feel shame and fear we think that the way back
to God is difficult, and that He is angry and ill-tempered
toward us, and that there is need of great preparation if we
wish to approach Him. But the loving-kindness of God utterly banishes this thought from the soul. What can prevent
anyone who clearly knows how kind He is and that, as it
is said, 'while you are yet speaking He will say, "Here I am" '

[Isaiah 58.9], from approaching Him at once for pardon of the sins which he has committed? This is a scheme and device against us on the part of our common enemy, that he moves him whom he leads into sin with rashness and daring, but inspires men with shame and groundless fear once they have ventured on the most terrible deeds. Thus in the former case he prepares their fall, in the latter he does not permit them to rise anew, but rather both leads them away from God and prevents them from returning to Him. So he leads to the same ruin by opposite paths.

It is necessary, then, to beware of these things with all eagerness, and to avoid the presumption before the sin no less than the shame and fear that follow it. They profit nothing, for this fear is not a spur to action but a stupor for our souls. We are not ashamed of our wounds in order that we may discover the means of healing, but rather in order that we may escape the eyes of the Savior like Adam who hid himself [Genesis 3.18]. On account of his wound he fled from the hand of the Physician whom he should have sought so that sin would not triumph over him; but by alleging his wife as an excuse he sought to cover up, as far as he could, the weakness of his will. After him Cain sought to be hidden by the means which he thought would hide him – and that from Him in whose sight are all things [Genesis 4.9]!

Now it is possible to have fear and shame and to humble one's soul and mortify one's body, and that with profit, when those things can lead to God. 'You will know them,' He says, 'by their fruits' [Matthew 7.20]. Now since grievous distress, even more than shame and fear, follows upon sin, no harm will come from this to those who rightly understand the loving-kindness of God. Even if they feel guilty of the ultimate wickedness they do not give up hope, knowing that no sin is too great for pardon or able to overcome God's kindness. They endure salutary grief and seek to increase it; other grief they reject since it outrages good hopes.

There are two kinds of grief for transgressions, one which restores those who are afflicted by it, and another which brings ruin upon them. Of both there are clear witnesses, the blessed Peter in the former case, the wretched Judas in the latter. The grief of the one preserved his purpose and commended him, after he wept bitterly to Christ no less than before he had sinned, whereas Judas' grief led him to the noose. When the blood was being shed which cleansed the whole world and all were being set free, he went off in bonds in despair of his own cleansing!

Since we know them beforehand let us welcome the former grief but flee from the latter. So we must look at the characteristics of both, how the former benefits us and the latter does us harm.

Because by sinning we commit an offense both against ourselves and against God, it will by no means harm us to grieve over our presumption against the Master; indeed, it would be most opportune. In the case of the other, when we have formed high opinions of ourselves we see them refuted by the acts whereby we have offended against our duty; we are pained and mourn, and sore remorse oppresses the heart as though life were not worth living for those who have fallen into such great evils. From this grief it is necessary to desist. It is clearly the mother of death, as is also excessive self-esteem.

The former kind of grief derives from affection towards our Master. It makes us clearly to know our Benefactor and the things for which we are indebted to Him. Of the things for which we are His debtors we have not repaid even one; on the contrary, we have requited Him with evil.

Therefore, just as pride is an evil, so the pain which comes to our souls from the latter grief is an evil. On the other hand the love of Christ is altogether worthy of praise. Nothing is more blessed to those who are well-disposed than to suffer pain by reason of the darts which come from that love and to pine away in soul.

Godly Sorrow Springs from Love of God

This is the way of the undefiled who, as the Psalmist says,

'seek Him with their whole heart' [Psalms 119.2], thereby
showing what is the desire which has been enjoined upon
us. Those who 'walk in the law of the Lord' [Psalms 119.1]
are those who live in love, the commandment on which the
whole law depends [Matthew 22.40]. They do so in order
that they may straightway strip themselves of all sin, which
alone obscures the vision of the soul. Nothing then impedes
them from looking towards right reason, even in their
desires, and from knowing clearly how much they ought
to lament.

As I have said before, the aim of human virtue is to share
in God's will, while the aim of wickedness is the opposite.
The former means that man attains his goal, the latter that
he falls short of it. When those who live philosophically for
reward are virtuous, it is not because they love virtue for
itself. When they fall from it they do not deplore sin on its
own account. They practise virtue because they desire
rewards and shun sin because of its penalty. Thus it is not
the substance of sin, so to speak, which they really hate,
and even when they have ceased from actively sinning they
do not really flee from it in the disposition of their will. Just
as he who hates wicked men cannot properly be called a
hater of mankind, so to feel abhorrence of sin merely
because it brings punishment on its perpetrator rather than
because it conflicts with God's laws is not to shun
wickedness itself but merely to flee from its punishment.
It is quite clear that were it possible to sin without peril to
oneself such men would not flee from evil

But those whose affection for God exalts them to a
philosophical life honor the law because they love its Giver.
When they have offended God they condemn themselves
and blame themselves for the sin itself and bewail it, not
because they were cheated of the rewards of virtue but
because their will was not in harmony with God.

When, therefore, the former have repented of their of-
fences they are not completely pure from evil in their souls.
They still must seek the due measure of wretchedness and

lamentation and labors for their offenses, while the latter, since they have cast out all disease, will be self-sufficient in this regard. Since sin has two aspects they flee from both. They have ceased from sinful action by penitence. Evil passion does not persist in them, nor any disposition to sin, since their passion for goodness and for God cleaves to their souls and does not permit them.

GREGORY PALAMAS[32]

Prayer and Compunction

For it is the case that if we cannot taste mental prayer, not even as it were with the slightest touch of our lips, and if we are dominated by passionate emotions, then we certainly stand in need of the physical suffering that comes from fasting, vigils and similar things, if we are to apply ourselves to prayer. This suffering alone mortifies the body's inclination to sin, and moderates and weakens the thoughts that provoke violent passions. Moreover, it is this which brings about within us the the start of holy compunction, through which both the stain of past faults is done away with and divine favor especially attracted, and which disposes one towards prayer. For 'God will not despise a bruised heart,' as David says; and according to Gregory the Theologian, 'God heals in no more certain way than through suffering.' This is why the Lord taught us in the Gospels that prayer can do great things when combined with fasting.

SYMEON OF THESSALONIKE[33]

The 50th Psalm

First they recite the 50th Psalm of confession and propitiation, as a petition of forgiveness of sins so that the Holy Spirit may not be taken away from us, but be renewed through humility and contrition of heart. We recite this psalm at the start of several services, since it speaks on the one hand of Adam and our whole race, and on the other of the Church gathered from the nations. The former was put to death because of lust and disobedience, the latter because at first she was unfaithful, committing adultery and spiritual murder like an apostate, but by God's mercy she was recalled and, receiving in abundance the Holy Spirit, was renewed.

KOSMAS THE AITOLOS[34]

The Time for Confession Is Now

What are we, my fellow Christians, just or sinners? If we're just, we're of good fortune and thrice-blessed; if we're sinners, now is the time to repent, to cease from doing evil and do what is good, because hell waits for us.

When will we repent? Not tomorrow or the day after, but today, because we don't know what will happen to us by tomorrow. Take care, my brethren, don't be infected with pride, don't commit murder, don't fornicate, don't swear, don't lie, don't slander, don't betray another, don't deck out your body, because it will be eaten by worms. But adorn the soul which is worth more than the whole world. Pray, fast, give alms, keep death before you, and hope for the time when you'll leave this false world and go to that eternal one.

Listen, my brethren, just as a rich man who has ten servants and dismisses and replaces one when he makes a mistake, so it is with our Lord. When the first order of angels fell, God commanded and the world was made, and he made us human beings to put us in the place of the angels.

The Wise Confessor

There was a young man who went to confession to one confessor for fifteen years. Going once again to confess, he discovered the confessor fornicating with a woman. He said to himself: 'O! Woe is me! I have been confessing to him for so many years and now I'll be damned. No matter how many sins he has forgiven me, they're all unforgiven.'

Saying this, he immediately left. On the way he became thirsty. Proceeding farther, he found some running water so clean that he remarked: 'If the water here is so clean, how much cleaner must it be at the fountain where it originates?'

He bent down and drank. Going on, he came to the fountain and he saw that the water was coming out of the mouth of a dog. He sighed and said: 'Woe is me! I have been polluted!'

Then an angel of the Lord said to him: 'Why were you not polluted when you first drank the water, and now that you have seen it coming from the mouth of a dog, you abhor it? I wonder, isn't the dog from God who created the sky, the earth, and everything? If the dog is unclean, don't be sad; the water isn't his. It is the same with the confessor who heard your confessions. Was the forgiveness perhaps his? It belongs to the Holy Spirit. Because he possessed the office of the priesthood, he was superior to kings and angels. What does it matter to you if he committed fornication? He is the mouth of the dog, so don't be sad. Whatever he forgave you is forgiven. Only go and prostrate yourself before him and ask for his forgiveness. He'll be judged by God.'

Then the angel disappeared. The man went back to the confessor and told him everything the angel had advised him. Hearing the whole narrative, the confessor wept, repented, and was saved.

We must find fault with ourselves, and then we'll be saved.

TIKHON OF ZADONSK[35]

The Loving Initiative

Since you came into the world for all, O Savior, therefore you came for me, for I am one of all. You came into the world to save sinners, therefore You came to save me

also, for I am one of the sinners. You came to find and to
save him who was lost, therefore You came to seek me too,
for I am one of the lost. O Lord, O my God and Creator!
I should have come to You as a transgressor of Your law.
I should have fallen at Your feet, cast myself down before
You, humbly begging forgiveness, pleading with You and
craving Your mercy. But You Yourself have come to me,
wretched and good-for-nothing servant that I am; my Lord
has come to me, His enemy and apostate; my Master has
come and has bestowed His love of mankind upon me.
Listen, my soul: God has come to us; our Lord has visited us.

Thus I stand before You, I for whose sake You came to
earth. Beholding in me nothing but my need of salvation,
You have come to seek me. For You so looked upon me that
my misfortune and my perdition became Your loss, my salvation Your gain. That I should be saved and should attain
eternal happiness, this You considered to be Your gain. For
Your generosity could not bear to see me in perdition; it im-
pelled You, Invisible One, to descend and seek me. Not a
mediator, not an angel, but You Yourself, my Lord, came
to me. You came to me, for I could not come to You. The
Shepherd had to come and to labor in order to find the sheep
lost in the hills. You showered upon me Your loving-kindness, my Lord. You sought me disinterestedly, my Shepherd.
You loved me without profit, O my God! This indeed is true
love: to love without profit, to do good without hope of
recompense. Thus did You love me, my Lover: You came
disinterestedly for my salvation.

How shall I repay Your generosity, O my Lover? How
shall I repay my God for all that He has given me? Had I
died a thousand times for Your sake, it would be as nothing.
For You are my Lord, my Creator and my God, and I am
but clay and ashes, a sinner and a worthless servant, de-
serving of all manner of deaths, not alone in time but in eternity. How shall I thank You, my Lord, my Lover, my Inter-
cessor, my Liberator, my Redeemer? How shall I reward
You, who did not spare Yourself, but for my sake gave

Yourself up to dishonor, insult, mockery, infamy; to be spat upon, condemned, scourged, wounded, crucified, put to death that I, poor wretch, should be made joyful? How shall I reward You? I who possess nothing that is my own except for my corruption, my impotence, my sin. My soul and body, my nature, is from You – Yours, but alas! corrupted and spoiled by me. The counsel of the Evil One and my own will have corrupted me. I shall offer You a grateful heart, and that alone You desire of me. But even this thing I cannot do without You. For without You I cannot know You, or without having known You, love You. Oh, how poor, how indigent I am! How weak, miserable, corrupt! Oh, how deeply my enemy has wounded, how he has broken me! But, O my Liberator, forgive me! For You have loved me and have given Yourself up for me. Forgive me, and enlighten me, that I may know You in whom is my life. Kindle the love of You in my heart, set my feet upon the rock, and straighten my steps, so that I may follow You, my Liberator and my only Leader, guiding me to heaven and to eternal life. Draw me after You, O burning love! Let us run the path You have trod! I will follow the scent of Your myrrh. For wherever You are, there shall I also be, I, the servant whom You have redeemed, so that I may behold Your glory. O Merciful, O Generous, O Lover of men, give me the heart that is able to follow You; guide me along Your ways, along the path of Your chosen ones; lead me after You by Your Holy Ghost! 'Your good spirit shall lead me into the right land.'

You have accomplished a deed so sublime that my mind cannot grasp it! You, the Lord, the King of Heaven and Earth, have come down from Heaven, and have given Yourself flesh of the Virgin Mother of God, and have suffered, have been crucified, have shed Your own blood, for me, for the sake of Your servant! What a sublime wonder! I believe and I confess, I acknowledge and I preach, and I marvel that so great a love has been shown me! O Lover of men, my Lover, grant me, a sinner, yet another favor, I humbly implore You: cleanse me of all my sins with Your precious blood, the blood You have shed for the sake of Your sinning servant. Confirm me in fear of You, and in love of You. Grant that I may follow in Your steps through faith and charity. And guard me by Your strength from my enemies, who seek to stay my feet and to turn me from You, O Redeemer. 'And Your mercy will follow me all the days of my life,' so that, being preserved by Your grace, I shall offer You thanksgiving, face to face, with Your chosen ones, and shall sing, and praise, and glorify You, with the Eternal Father and the Holy Ghost, for ever and ever. Amen.

Advice for Priests

When giving instruction on the sacrament of repentance, the priest should speak to the penitent in this manner: 'My child, you are confessing to God, who is displeased at any sin; and I, His servant, am the unworthy witness of your repentance. Do not conceal anything, do not be ashamed or afraid, for there are only three of us here, you and I and God, before whom you have sinned, who knows all your sins and how they were committed. God is everywhere, and wherever you said, thought, or did anything evil, He was there and knew all about it; and He is here with us now, and is waiting for your words of confession and repentance. You, too, know all your sins: do not be ashamed to speak of all that you have committed. And I, who am here, am a sinner just like you; so then, do not be ashamed to confess your sins in my presence.'

NIKODEMOS OF ATHOS[36]

Against Despair for Sins

If you happen to fall into some pardonable transgression by word or deed – for example, if you are perturbed by some accidental happening, or criticize, or listen to criticisms by others, or enter into argument about something, or are at times impatient, flustered, or suspicious of others, or if you neglect something, you must not be too perturbed, sorrowful, and despairing in thinking about what you have done; above all you must not aggravate your perturbation by sad thoughts about yourself: that evidently you will never manage to free yourself of such weaknesses, that your will to work for the Lord is too weak, or that you are not progressing on the path of God as you should. For every time you do this you burden your soul with thousands of other fears produced by faintness of heart and sadness.

Even if you go to confession, you do so with a disturbing fear, and after confession you still find no peace, for it seems that you have not said everything. Thus you live a life that is bitter, disquieted and of little fruit, and you waste much time uselessly. And all this happens because we forget our natural weakness and lose sight of the attitude the soul must have to God. In other words, we forget that when the soul falls into some pardonable sin that is not mortal, it should turn to God with humble repentance and hope, and not torture itself with excessive sorrow, bitterness and stress.

Repentance must always be inspired and imbued with firm trust in God, and still more must it be so in sins more grievous than ordinary, into which even a zealous servant of God sometimes falls by God's leave. For penitent distress which so tortures the heart and gnaws at it can never reestablish hope in the soul, if it is not accompanied by a firm trust in divine goodness and mercy. This trust must always fill the heart of those wishing to reach the highest degrees of Christian perfection. It animates and tautens all the powers of the soul and the spirit. Yet many who have entered the path of spiritual life fail to pay attention to this, and so stop in their progress with heart weakened, and move no further; thus they become unsuitable for receiving the blessings of grace, which the Lord has distributed along this path and which usually reward only those whose efforts never slacken and who move steadfastly on and on.

But above all, those who experience some perturbation

of the heart, or some perplexity, or a split in their conscience,
must turn to their spiritual Father or someone else experienced in spiritual life, at the same time trustfully begging
the Lord to reveal the truth through them and send them
a reassuring solution of their troubles and perplexities.
Thereupon a man should be wholly set at rest by their word.

IGNATII BRIANCHANINOV

The Necessary Foundation for Spiritual Life

From the fallen human spirit God accepts only one
sacrifice – repentance. Other sacrifices, even the strictest
asceticism such as might be called a whole burnt offering
or holocaust, are rejected as being defiled by sin and need-
ing purification by repentance before they can be offered
in sacrifice. This is the one sacrifice of fallen man which
God does not despise by refusing it. When Zion is renewed
by repentance and the walls of our spiritual Jerusalem are
built, then we can confidently offer on the altar of our heart
sacrifices of righteousness – our sentiments and feelings
renewed by the grace of God. Then a person becomes fit
to offer even himself as a holocaust pleasing to God. The
holy martyr Sadok said, 'Whoever is spiritual awaits a martyr's death with joy, longing, and great love; he is not afraid
of it because he is ready. But to a carnal person the hour
of death is terrible.'

Repentance is a commandment of the Gospel. The immediate consequence of repentance, according to the Gospel,
should be our entry into the kingdom of heaven. Therefore
the whole space of time from our adoption by Christ till our
entry into eternity (and the heavenly kingdom becomes the
secure possession of those who are granted salvation), or
the whole of our earthly life, should be a field of repentance.
The first sermon and commandment uttered by God incarnate to our fallen humanity which He came to save was
about repentance: Jesus began to preach and say, 'Repent

for the kingdom of heaven is at hand.' After His Resurrection and before His Ascension to heaven, the Lord opened the Apostles' minds and enabled them to understand the Scriptures. Then He told them that, in accordance with the Scriptures, it was inevitable that Christ should suffer and rise from the dead on the third day, and that repentance and forgiveness of sins should be preached in His name to all nations, beginning from Jerusalem.

Vision of Oneself

The greatest of the holy Fathers admitted that repentance was their sole occupation. Having given themselves up to this activity, they more and more widened its scope for themselves, since repentance not only cleanses a person from sins but also sharpens his sight so that he sees himself more clearly. When some spots of sin are removed from the garment of the soul by repentance, then suddenly the existence of other spots is discovered, less coarse but no less important, which have remained unnoticed till now on account of the dullness of our sight. Finally repentance leads a person who practices it to the most profound spiritual visions; there is disclosed to him his own fall and the fall of all mankind, his suffering and the suffering of mankind under the yoke of the prince of this world, the wonderful work of redemption and the other mysteries; with which the reader must become acquainted by experience, for human speech is quite inadequate to tell of them.

Examples of Continual Weeping

Saint Arsenios the Great had repentance as his constant occupation, and it was so much a part of him that it expressed itself in the gift of tears. A handkerchief was always on his lap, and while his hands were busy with work and his mind occupied in penitential prayer, tears fell continually on his handkerchief. Saint Sisoes the Great asked the angels, who came to take his soul from his body to carry it to heaven, to leave him in his body and give him time for repentance. And to his disciples who were sure he had reached perfection he said that he did not know whether he had really begun to repent. So high a conception had he of repentance! Evidently the saint here called the whole of his life repentance, and by saying that he had not yet begun his repentance he expressed the humble opinion he had of his own life.

Those who have acquired a true, spiritual understanding of repentance include it in all their labors, prayer, and fasting, and consider it a day lost on which they have not wept over themselves, whatever other good works they may have done notwithstanding. There is no doubt that Saint Sisoes was immersed in the work of repentance and weeping. One of the properties of this work is that the penitent can never be satisfied, but the more it fills him, the more he longs for it, since it procures a purity most pleasing to God and at the same time produces a thirst for a still more perfect purity. Those who are purified by weeping see how impure they are and continue to acknowledge their impurity.

The way to attain compunction is an attentive life. The beginning of repentance comes from the fear of God and attention, as the holy martyr Boniface says. The fear of God is the father of attention, and attention is the mother of inner peace, which gives birth to a conscience which enables the soul to see its deformity as in a kind of clear and still water; and so are born the beginnings and roots of repentance. An attentive and regular life according to the commandments of the Gospel, even though it is the first cause of repentance, yet so long as it is not overshadowed by divine grace and is without fruit, will not produce heartfelt contrition, compunction, mourning, tears, all of which constitute true (monastic) repentance.

Demonic Deceptions and the Struggle of the Christian

The spiritual way of repentance and mourning has such

power that it is immune to demonic deception, so-called diabolic deception. The fallen spirit, in order to dupe the ascetic, first tries to convince him of his worth or merits . . . but how can he dupe a person who seeks with all his power to discover his sinfulness, who bewails what has been revealed to him and is roused by it to seek further insights, whose sole endeavor is to see in himself the one and only plea of a sinner, so that both by his outer and inner activity he may offer to God the realisation and confession of his sinfulness. 'When the devil,' says Saint Gregory the Sinaite, 'sees someone living a life of mourning, he does not stay near him, being repelled by his humility born of weeping.' Though the devil does also tempt those who mourn, yet he is easily recognized by them and repulsed. A self-opinionated person who thinks he has some worth or merit cannot repulse the devil's seduction from without, because he is possessed and chained by him from within.

Ignorant and quack ascetics think they have reached their goal when they see themselves saints, when the world thinks and proclaims them such. They rejoice at the self-deception and self-opinion that has got into them, not understanding how fatal self-deception is, not realizing that human praise is the sign of a false prophet. This sign is extremely important. It is given by the God-Man Himself. 'Woe!' said the Lord, 'woe betide you when all men speak well of you! For this is exactly what their fathers did to the false prophets' [Luke 6.26]. Woe, spiritual woe and disaster, eternal misery!

A true (monk) rejoices when he begins to see his sin, when in his own opinion of himself he becomes lower and more sinful than all his neighbors, when he begins to shake with fear at the thought of God's judgement and the eternal torments, when he feels like a criminal and convict, when during his prayers torrents of tears begin to flow and sighs and groans burst from his breast, when his mind purified by tears stands before God face to face, and he sees the Invisible by means of a vivid sense of the presence of God. O blessed vision! In this light the criminal or delinquent can offer true repentance for the crimes or offenses committed by him; he can move the All-Merciful to mercy by his abundant tears, by humble words and by laying bare his woeful condition; he can ask the compassionate God for forgiveness, and therewith also for a multitude of priceless, eternal, spiritual gifts. One's greatest success is to see and acknowledge that he is a sinner. It is a great success when he proves by all his actions that he really and sincerely admits that he is a sinner.

A Gift from Above

The mind can see its sins when the grace of God touches it. Darkened by the fall, of itself it is incapable of seeing them. The sight of our sins and our sinfulness is a gift of God. The holy Orthodox Church teaches her children to ask God for this gift with fasting and prostrations, especially during the days of holy Lent. The gift of seeing our sins, our fallen state, the fellowship or intercourse of fallen man with the fallen angels, was inconceivably abundant in the great holy Fathers; in spite of the abundance of their spiritual gifts which clearly bore evidence to their holiness, it urged them to unceasing repentance and mourning, to a continual washing of themselves with their tears. The sayings of the Fathers from this state or level are incomprehensible to carnal minds. This, Poimen the Great used to say to the brethren who lived with him: 'Brothers! Believe me, where Satan will be thrown I shall be thrown too. Everyone who exalts himself will be humbled, but he who humbles himself will be exalted,' said the Lord [Luke 18.14].

THEOPHAN THE RECLUSE[38]

Christ Within Us Through the Sacraments

You are making strenuous efforts to attain the habit of the Jesus Prayer. May the Lord bless you! You must believe that the Lord Jesus Christ is within us, by the power of baptism and holy Communion, according to His own promise; for He is united with us through these sacraments. For those who are baptized are clothed in Christ, and those who take holy Communion receive the Lord. 'He that eateth my flesh and drinketh my blood dwelleth in me, and I in him,' says the Lord [John 6.56]. Only mortal sins deprive us of this great mercy, and even then it can be regained by those who repent and go to confession and afterwards receive holy Communion. You must believe this. If your faith is insufficient, pray that God may increase it and establish it in you, firm and unshakeable.

Continual Awareness

It is impossible to live at peace with God without continual repentance. The Apostle John lays down the following condition for peace with God: 'If our heart condemn us not' [1 John 3.21]. If you have nothing on your conscience, you can have boldness of access to God with a feeling of peace; but if you have something, then the peace is disturbed. To have something on our conscience: this is due to the awareness of sin. But according to the same Apostle we are never without sin, and he feels this so strongly that he calls anyone who imagines otherwise a liar [1 John 1.8]. Consequently, there is never a single moment when we have nothing on our conscience, either voluntary or involuntary, and therefore there is never a single moment when our peace with God is assured. It follows from this that it is absolutely essential to cleanse our conscience in order to be at peace with God. The conscience is cleansed by repentance; consequently, it is necessary to repent unceasingly. For repentance cleanses all pollution from the soul and makes it pure [1 John 1.9]. Repentance does not just consist in the words, 'Forgive, O Lord. Have mercy, O Lord.' To receive remission of sins we must also realize to the full the definite impurity of each thought, glance, and word, of every kind of allurement; we must be conscious of our own guilt and of our own lawlessness and absence of justification; we must recognize our need to pray for God's forgiveness until the spirit attains peace. As far as great sins are concerned, they must be confessed immediately to our spiritual father and pardon obtained, because in the case of such sins we cannot restore peace to our spirit simply by daily acts of repentance in our private prayers. Therefore the duty of continual repentance is the same as the duty of keeping our conscience pure and irreproachable.

SERGEJ BULGAKOV[39]

The Doors of Penitence

The Church is praying today for the opening of the doors of penitence. What are these doors? Where are they to be found? How often we complain and bewail that we know no repentance, that we cannot and do not know how to repent! The heart remains cold and empty even when we seek repentance, and our mind remains drowsy. And yet we know that without repentance there is no salvation. Apart from it we cannot draw near to God's kingdom; there can be no living faith without it. It is the salt of faith. How are we to enter into the force of it?

Repentance begins by consciously seeing and knowing our sin: 'For I acknowledge my transgressions, and my sin is ever before me' – thus the soul testified of itself in the Psalmist's penitential lamentation [Psalm 50]. A man may not be conscious of his sin at all, being in complete bondage to it. The soul may be sunk in deep, death-like sleep, and if it does not wake the sleep will prove to be the sleep of real spiritual death. So long as men remain unconscious of sin, they hate in their heathen blindness the very word 'sin' and feel angry irritation at the thought of it. The soul is vaguely aware that it means condemnation of its whole past and a call to renewal: 'Repent you and believe the Gospel' [Mark 1.15], and our selfishness and inertia resist this call.

Without repentance the natural man cannot be born as a spiritual man. So this is the first door of repentance: knowledge of one's sin and of oneself as possessed by it. A ray suddenly lightens the soul's darkness, and in its light man sees himself before the face of God. The eye of God beholds us through our conscience, which is God's testimony of Himself in the soul of man. Conscience judges us with true, righteous, and incorrupt judgement, and its present judgement is as it were an anticipation of Christ's Last Judgement. It is the greatest gift of divine love which God has bestowed on man, for what can be 'more needful than conscience?' (– the words of Saint Andrew of Crete). Through conscience we see ourselves in the light of divine truth: 'that you might be justified when you speak and be clear when you judge' [Psalm 50]. This priceless gift of God is entrusted to everyone, not only to Christians, but to the Gentiles as well. The first impulse of the soul, when in the light of conscience it sees itself in its sin, is to hide from the face of God in the shadow of the trees, like Adam and Eve in the garden of Eden, when they saw their nakedness. Calm self-complacency and proud self-satisfaction disappear and are replaced by shame, confusion, and even fear at the things that have been revealed to man about himself. This is a difficult and dangerous 'hour before daybreak,' because usually at this point cowardly depression and profound disappointment in ourselves lie in wait for us. The force of repentance draws us, however, not into a passive contemplation of sin, but to active struggle against it. Repentance forces us to seek deliverance from sin, purification: 'make in me a clean heart, O God, and renew a right spirit within me,' prays the soul together with the Psalmist [Psalms 50.10].

At this point the work of penitence begins, apart from which salvation cannot be attained; it begins but it has no end, for it is lifelong. Without this work there is no active penitence but only a vague wish for it. And this is the second door of repentance. Woe to us if we confine ourselves to the knowledge of sin and, refusing the effort, avoid direct struggle against it: such a man 'has no cloak for his sin' [John 15.22]. But self-knowledge leads to self-reproach, and self-reproach to fresh self-knowledge. The depths of the heart are opened more and more, new sins come to memory, and at the very bottom the serpent of original sin writhes its coils. Spiritual labor united with self-scrutiny does not, however, lead to weakness or depression, but strengthens one's courage, renews the powers of the soul, and is like salt for it. A penitent goes on working away, unobserved, in a state of spiritual alertness which is reflected in his whole life. And he has his solace, for the heavenly Father gives him bounties in the sacrament of penance, gives him the joy of forgiveness. 'Restore to me the joy of Your salvation, and uphold me with Your free spirit,' the penitent soul repeats with the Psalmist [Psalms 50.12]. The work of penitence is the heart of all works, and this is why in great ascetics it is accompanied by a gracious blossoming of all their spiritual powers. Through penitence the nature of man as originally created is liberated from the distortions of sin. It was in order to manifest to sinners the salutary fruits of penitence that the Lord granted the remission of sins in the sacrament of penance. Through it the past becomes non-existent, the stripes of sin are healed by the power of Christ. But only that which has been found by man in his own heart, condemned, and fought against, can thus be wiped out. Man must himself open the sad pages in his book of life that they may be deleted through the grace of the sacrament; un-repented sins are not wiped out. True penitence is useful in every way: it gives healing and health, peace and joy, humility and courage, sobriety and watchfulness. Through enmity to sin it strengthens our love for God and testifies to it. We need the power of penitence at all times, but the holy Church has singled out and blessed the days of Lent as a special season for it. And, behold, now our souls are called to it by the prayer, 'Open to me the doors of penitence, O Life-Giver.'

ALEXANDER ELCHANINOV[40]

Advice for Confession

'Behold, now is the day of salvation' [2 Corinthians 6.2]. Now is the time for us to lay aside the heavy burden of sin, to break its chains, and to behold once more the 'fallen and shattered tabernacle' of our soul, renewed and radiant. But the way which leads to this blessed purification is far from easy.

We have not yet begun to prepare for confession, and already our soul hears the voices of temptation: 'Should I put it off? Am I sufficiently prepared, am I not making these special fasts and acts of preparation too often?' We must firmly resist these doubts. 'If you come to serve the Lord, prepare your soul for temptation' [Ecclesiasticus 2.1]. If you have decided to make this special act of preparation, you must expect to encounter many obstacles, interior and exterior; but they vanish as soon as you show firmness in your intentions.

Confession is not just a talk about your faults and doubts, it is not a way of telling your confessor all about yourself, and least of all is it a 'pious practice.' Confession is an act of fervent, heartfelt repentance, a thirst for purification; it springs from an awareness of what is holy, it means dying to sin and coming alive again to sanctity. Contrition is in itself already a measure of sanctity. Insensibility and unbelief mean that we are outside sanctity.

Undoubtedly, the first act is a searching of the heart. That is why the days of preparation have been instituted. 'To see your sins, in all their multiplicity and hideousness, this is indeed a gift of God,' writes John of Kronstadt. People inexperienced in the spiritual life usually see neither the number of their sins nor their 'hideousness.' 'Nothing in particular,' 'like everyone else,' 'only petty sins,' 'I have neither stolen nor killed': such is the usual beginning of confession by many penitents. And what about pride, refusal to suffer reproaches, hardness of heart, slander, weakness of faith and love, faintheartedness, spiritual sloth; are these not serious sins?

This is why the shortest way to attain a knowledge of our sin is to draw nearer to the light and to pray for that light which judges the world and all that is 'worldly' in ourselves [John 3.19]. As long as we lack that closeness to Christ which makes the feeling of repentance our habitual condition, we must prepare for confession by an examination of conscience according to the commandments, by certain prayers (for instance, the third of the evening prayers, the fourth of the prayers before Communion), and by texts from Scripture (for instance, Romans 5.12, Ephesians 4, and James, especially chapter 3).

Preparation for confession does not consist in recalling your sins as fully as possible and even writing them down. It means striving to attain such a state of concentration, seriousness and prayer that your sins will become as clear as if they had been exposed to the light. In other words, you should bring to your confessor not a list of sins but a feeling of repentance, not a minutely studied dissertation but a contrite heart.

But to know your sins does not yet mean to repent of them. True, our Lord accepts a sincere, conscientious confession even though it is not accompanied by a feeling of repentance (if we courageously confess as well this sin of 'petrified sensibility'). However, contrition of the heart, sorrow for our sins, is the most important thing that we can bring to confession. But what are we to do if our heart, 'dried up with sin,' is not watered by the vivifying stream of tears? What if 'weakness of soul and frailty of body' are so great that we are incapable of sincere repentance? All the same, this is no reason for putting off confession. God may touch our hearts during the confession itself. The very confession, the naming of our sins, may soften our hearts, refine our spiritual sight, sharpen the feeling of repentance.

The third stage of repentance is the oral confession of sins. Do not wait to be questioned, make an effort for yourself; confession is a courageous feat of self-constraint. You must speak with precision, without veiling the ugliness of sin by vague expressions (as, for instance, 'I have sinned against the seventh commandment'). It is very difficult in confession to avoid the temptation of self-justification: we try to put before the confessor 'extenuating circumstances,' and make allusions to a 'third person' who led us into sin. All this is a mark of vanity, indicating the absence of deep repentance and a continued stagnation in sin.

VASILIOS OF STAVRONIKITA[41]

An Example of Repentance as Love

Here is something very characteristic. An old monk, a true ascetic, comes to our monastery from time to time to ask for a little help. With what he receives, he feeds himself and also helps others, older than himself.

One day he came for his usual visit and said to one of the brethren of the monastery, 'I hope that I am not being too much trouble to you, coming and asking for your help. If I am too much bother, don't worry yourself, I needn't come again. Don't worry about it: a monk is like a dog. If you give him a kick, it does him good; and if you don't give him a kick, but a piece of bread instead, this does him good as well.'

The old man, although he is more than seventy-five years old, does not expect anyone to respect him. He thinks of himself as a dog. He bows to everyone and asks his blessing, not only to the monks but also to the novices and to the pilgrims who come to us. But he is full of such inexpressible grace that a joyful sense of celebration runs through the monastery every time he comes. All of us, monks and pilgrims, gather round him to hear the words of grace that come from his lips, to be encouraged by the joy that his face reflects, without him ever suspecting it. It is like that Father of the desert who asked God that he might not receive any glory on this earth, and whose face was so radiant that no one could look directly at him.

In humble men like this, who radiate grace, one feels that

two great virtues are always at work: the mystery of repentance and the mystery of love. They are not men who have been converted, who have repented. They are men who are being converted, who are repenting. The Lord's call to repentance does not mean that we are to be converted once only, nor that we should repent from time to time (though one ought to begin with that). It means that our whole life should be a conversion, a constant repentance, that in us there should always be a state of repentance and contrition. We ought not to speak or think or do anything outside that atmosphere, that attitude of penitence and contrition which should fill our whole being.

At every moment this mystery of penitence, of contrition, of being raised up by the power of Another, should be at work in us. At every moment, being cast down, we feel ourselves raised up by Another. We feel that we are fallen and He is the Resurrection, that we are non-being and He is Being itself. It is by His infinite mercy that He brought us from non-being into being, and when we were fallen He raised us up, and He continues to raise us up at every moment. Thus, as the spirit of repentance grows within us, we are led to say with the Apostle: 'We carry in our body the dying of the Lord Jesus, that the life of the Lord Jesus may also be manifest in our body' [2 Corinthians 4.10]. Those who can say this live at one and the same time Good Friday and Easter Day. They constantly live the 'life-giving death' of the Lord, the 'sorrow which brings joy.'

What they experience in their repentance they experience also through sharing in the mystery of love. In love also they see the way of sacrifice that leads directly and surely to eternal life. No effort which is offered out of love for God remains in vain. Everything which is offered and given up for love of the brethren is saved, kept intact, multiplied in eternal life.

Our neighbor is not simply an indispensible companion on the way of life. He is an integral part of our spiritual existence. Only in losing himself for God and for his fellowman, his brother, can man find the true dimension of his own life. 'He who loses . . . finds.' Only thus can the true glory of the human person be restored to him, a glory at once divine and human, without limits. Only in this way can a man feel within himself that the foundations on which he builds are unshaken. These foundations are death, annihilation. The anthropological reality in which the new man lives from henceforth is the divine grace which embraces all things.

The reward given for the glass of water offered to our brother is the new Trinitarian consciousness which comes to birth within us. The other one is no longer the frontier which determines our individuality, which closes off our own living space, or simply flatters our complacency. He is not the shroud which envelopes our deadly isolation. He is not hell. The other is the true place of our life, he is my most dear and irreplaceable self who gives me here and now, through my gift of myself to him, the meaning and reality of eternal life, an eternal life which has already begun. As the beloved disciple says, 'We know that we have passed from death to life because we love the brethren' [1 John 3.14].

EPILOGUE:
ARCHIMANDRITE AIMILIANOS[42]

The Spiritual Father in the Monastery

A monastery is not a human society, but a continuous gathering of the brotherhood — in the church, in the refectory, at the various times it meets. It is a gathering which is one with the forward movement of the Church itself through the course of its history. It is an expression of the entire gathering of the Church, reproducing the prototype of this brotherhood as it was given to us by Christ and his Apostles. This included not only visible members, but also all those who would take their place beside them to make up the Church of the past and of the future. A monastery is therefore a symbol of the Church in its totality. It is the

gathering of the Church itself concentrated and focused in
one small place. The spiritual father (*gerontas*), the hegumen,
or abbot, of the monastery, is thus, in some sense, an image
of God; he represents Christ, and the rest of the monks form
the communion of saints, both the living and the dead.

A monastery is a mystery, a sacrament, and its spiritual
father is part of the visible element of this mystery, behind
which is hidden the invisible: God and all that is not seen
and can only be perceived by the intellect.

The important position of the spiritual father, lying as
it does at the very heart of the mystery, means also that he
guides these men, that he fashions them with his own hands
so as to incorporate them bodily into the life of the Church
and of Christ.

The monastic superior, then, is not concerned only with
everyday life, with the food and material needs of the community: above all, he is a guide of souls, initiating them into
the mysteries, showing them the path to perfect mystical
union with God.

It must be understood that the monastery is a very special
kind of community. It belongs, in fact, to Paradise, to the
kingdom of heaven. It is a communion of saints, in which
each believer, in this case each monk, enjoys unlimited right
to the life of Christ, and where Christ himself has the same
right to the life of each person. The monastery constitutes,
therefore, a very important aspect of reality, since it pre-
serves the rights which man possessed before the Fall, that is,
the possibility of possessing God wholly as his own. It is this
reality that the hegumen must realize and demonstrate daily
to his monks, that is, to the disciples of the Lord himself.

He is a master, then, who passes on to them what he
knows, but who must above all show them, through his own
life, a knowledge of the true God – through the fire that
he kindles in their hearts and the understanding that he gives
them, so that they are aware of Christ as everywhere present and as the Promised One. For, whatever may be his daily
activities, the monk's life is nothing other than a zealous and

impatient expectation of God.

Gradually, the spiritual father will take the monk and raise him to higher things, so that he is given divine grace. For in the mystical life it is grace which accomplishes everything, and Christ is not only the Promised One, but also a person to whom one can speak. In this way the monk learns to dedicate himself to his Master, the Lord Jesus Christ, and to have just the same intimacy and friendship with him as did the circle of the Apostles. And finally, thanks to his daily efforts, and to the attentive care of the Holy Trinity, the hegumen will be able to achieve another result: the monks will perceive God as a living Being, coexisting with them, and accompanying them in everything they do, from the time they awaken, as they walk about the monastery, and in the smallest glance. Then there will be full communion between God and man.

Thus it is the spiritual father who takes his disciple, the monk, by the hand and presents him to the Lord. It is he who makes Christ come down, who reunites that which was separated – the realms of heaven and of earth – so as to transform them into a single true and unique dance.

Such is the true role of the spiritual father, and this is how the monks see him. And this is why there is this discipline and obedience, this love, this gift of self, this trust, all of which are not directed to the superior as man, but to Christ whom he represents.

All the monks share this sense of the mystery and the mystical reality of which is manifest among them, for the Elder is not a new phenomenon in the monastery: he comes forth from the broad stream of Orthodox Tradition, he springs from the flow of the Holy Spirit.

Although he is only a man, within the framework of the monastic life the perception of his humanity tends to disappear. To be sure, he lives quite like everyone else; but he is also someone who has been taken and set apart by God, and as a result he no longer lives like someone who belongs to this world. For although he walks on the earth, he feels, in a way, that his head is in heaven, that he sees heaven, that he sees God. This is the most important thing that a monastery can offer. What society and modern man most lack is made so perceptible, so powerful, so alive, so intense, and so authentic by the spiritual father.

Therefore the monastic community around its spiritual father is in this way an image of the universal Church in its entirety. Everyday life is very simple in the monastery, but in the silence and tranquility which are brought into being by harmony and mutual love, men stand on tip toe, hoping to discern the gentle sound of Christ's approaching steps.

NOTES

[1]Clement of Rome, *Epistles*, in *Early Christian Fathers* (New York, 1970), pp. 47 and 200; also *Epistle to the Romans 2*, 8-9, PG 1.324A-44A.

[2]*On Repentance*, in *The Faith of the Early Fathers, 2* (Collegeville, 1970), pp. 130-31; *On the Soul 41*, in *The Early Christian Fathers* (Oxford, 1978), p. 117.

[3]*Quis Dives Salvetur 39* and 41, PG 9.644C-45A and 652A; *Paedagogus 9*, PG 8.548C.

[4]*On Prayer 28*, in *Classics of Western Spirituality* (London, 1979), p. 150; *Homily on Luke 17*, in *The Early Christian Fathers* (Oxford, 1978), p. 253.

[5]*Letter to Marcellinus*, in *Classics of Western Spirituality* (London, 1980), pp. 111 and 118.

[6]*Ad Theodorum Lapsum 1*, 6 and 8, PG 47.284 and 286; *Contra Virginum Corruptores*, PG 60.742.

[7]*Longer Rules 1*, PG 31.892A and *Morals*, in *The Fathers of the Church* (Boston, 1950), p. 9.

[8]*Life of Moses 2*, in *Classics of Western Spirituality* (New York, 1978), pp. 74, 123-24.

[9]*Conference 2*, in *Classics of Western Spirituality* (New York, 1985), pp. 69-70.

[10]In A. M. Coniaris, *These Are the Sacraments* (Minneapolis, 1981), p. 78.

[11]*Confessions 10*, in *Classics of Western Spirituality* (London, 1984), pp. 122-25.

[12 a)] *Sayings of the Desert Fathers* (London, 1975), pp. 20, 60, 65, 103, 121, 127, 142, 150, 155-56, 174, 180, 182, 185, 188-89.

[b)] *Wisdom of the Desert Fathers* (Oxford, 1975), pp. 39-40.

[c)] *The Paradise of the Fathers* (Seattle), pp. 32, 34, 139-40.

[13] *Philokalia 1* (London, 1979), p. 221.

[14] *Philokalia 1* (London, 1979), p. 129 and PG 65.940D, 952D. Also *On Repentance* 1, 6-7, 11-12, PG 65.965B, 973D-76B, 980D-81D.

[15] *Letters* 170 and 543. Last quotation from *Lausiac History* 140, PG 34.1241BC.

[16] *Gnostic Chapters* 17.

[17] *Spiritual Meadow* 59, 110, and 159, PG 87 (3).2912C, 2973B, and 3028AB.

[18] *Logos* 8, 16, and 25.

[19] *Philokalia 1* (London, 1979), p. 318.

[20] *Philokalia 1*)London, 1979), pp. 183-84 and 189.

[21] *Philokalia 2* (London, 1981), p. 369-70 and p. 27.

[22] *Philokalia 3* (London, 1984), p. 35.

[23] *Philokalia 3* (London, 1984), pp. 84, 160, 170, 199, 202, and 223.

[24] *Philokalia 4* (Athens, 1976), p. 275 [in Greek].

[25] *The Rule of St Benedict* (Collegeville, 1981), pp. 185 and 201.

[26] *Pastoral Care*, Part 3, 30 (Westminster, 1950), pp. 206-07.

[27] *Mystic Treatises*, ed. A. J. Wensinck (Wiesbaden, 1922), pp. 75-76, 164-65, 170, 210, 240-41, 273-74, 297-99, 310, 335, 337, 368.

[28] *Chapters on Love* 2, 81, in *Classics of Western Spirituality* (London, 1985), p. 58.

[29] *The Ladder of Divine Ascent*, in *Classics of Western Spirituality* (London, 1982), pp. 121-31.

[30 a)] *Discourses* 3 and 28, *Theological and Ethical Treatises* 2.

[b)] *The Discourses*, in *Classics of Western Spirituality (London, 1980), pp. 83, 90-94, 196-97, 298-99.*

[c)] *The Sin of Adam* (Platina, 1979), pp. 84-85.

[31] *The Life in Christ* (New York, 1974), pp. 167-70, 209-10.

[32] *Triads* 2, 2, 6, in *Classics of Western Spirituality* (London, 1983), p. 49.

[33] Symeon of Thessalonike, *Treatise on Prayer* trans. H. L. N. Simmons (Brookline, 1977), p. 24.

[34] N. M. Vaporis, *Father Kosmas, the Apostle to the Poor*

(Brookline, 1977), pp. 33-34, 139.

[35]In G. P. Fedotov, *A Treasury of Russian Spirituality* (Norland, 1975), pp. 216, 218, 223-24; N. Gorodetzky *Saint Tikhon Zadonsky* (London, 1951), pp. 126-27.

[36]*Unseen Warfare* (revised edition by Theophan the Recluse, London, 1978), pp. 277-79.

[37]*The Arena* (reprinted Jordanville, 1982), pp. 230-31, 234-45, 238, 242-44.

[38]In Timothy Ware, ed., *The Art of Prayer: An Orthodox Anthology* (London, 1966), pp. 173, 227-28.

[39]*Sergius Bulgakov: A Bulgakov Anthology* (London, 1976), pp. 175-77.

[40]*The Diary of a Russian Priest* (London, 1967), pp. 232-37.

[41]*Hymn of Entry* (New York, 1984), pp. 123-25.

[42]In *Sourozh* 27 (1987) 21-23.

SELECT BIBLIOGRAPHY

The following are short but valuable studies on repentance which include further sources for the reader.

Kallistos, Bishop (Ware), 'The Orthodox Experience of Repentance,' *Sobornost/Eastern Churches Review* 2,1 (1980), 18-28.

Kniazeff, Fr A., 'On the Sacrament of Repentance,' *Sourozh* 20 (1985), 27-31.

Stylianos, Archbishop (Harkianakis), 'Repentance and Confession,' *Akropolis Newspaper* (Athens), 10-4-80, 1and 6.

Voulgarakis, E., "Intimations on the Theme of Repentance," *Synaxi* 21 (Athens) 51-58.

SERVICE OF THE PENITENTS

Priest:

Blessed is our God always, now and forever, and to the ages of ages.

In peace let us pray to the Lord.

For peace from God and the salvation of our souls, let us pray to the Lord.

For the remission of sins, the forgiveness of the faults of the servant of God (*Name*) and that he (*she*) may be forgiven every fault voluntary and involuntary, let us pray to the Lord.

That the Lord may grant him (*her*) remission of sins and time for repentance, let us pray to the Lord.

Help us, save us, comfort and protect us, O God, by Your grace.

Remembering our most holy, pure, blessed and glorious Lady, the Theotokos, and ever-virgin Mary with all the saints, let us commit ourselves and one another and our whole life to Christ our God.

For to You belong all glory, honor, and worship, to the Father and the Son and the Holy Spirit, now and forever and to the ages of ages. Amen.

Let us pray to the Lord:

O Lord Jesus Christ, Son of the Living God, shepherd and lamb, who takes away the sin of the world; who did remit the loan to the two debtors, and did grant remission of her sins to the sinful woman: the same Lord, do loose,

95

remit, forgive the sins, transgressions, and iniquities, voluntary and involuntary, committed in guilt and disobedience by these Your servants. And if they, as men (*women*) bearing flesh and living in the world, have in any way been beguiled by the devil in word or deed, in knowledge or ignorance, despising the word of a priest or falling under his anathema, or breaking of their oath, You, the same good and forgiving Master, graciously free these Your servants by Your word, forgiving them their anathema and curse according to Your great mercy. Yes, gracious Master and Lord, hear us who make our petitions to Your goodness on behalf of these Your servants, and as Your are most merciful, overlook all their faults and free them from eternal damnation. For You have said, O Master: 'Whatsoever you shall bind on earth shall be bound in heaven, and whatsoever you shall loose on earth shall be loosed in heaven.' For You alone are sinless, and to You we give glory, with Your unoriginate Father and Your all-holy, good and life-giving Spirit, now and forever and to the ages of ages. Amen.

Holy God, Holy Mighty, Holy Immortal, have mercy on us (3).

Glory to the Father and the Son and the Holy Spirit, now and forever and to the ages of ages. Amen.

Most Holy Trinity, have mercy upon us. Lord, pardon our sins. Master, Forgive our iniquities. Holy One, visit and heal our infirmities, for Your Name's sake. Lord, have mercy. Lord, have mercy. Lord, have mercy.

Glory to the Father and the Son and the Holy Spirit, now and forever and to the ages of ages. Amen.

Our Father, who art in heaven, hallowed be Thy name. Thy kingdom come; Thy will be done, on earth as it is in heaven. Give us this day our daily bread. And forgive us our trespasses, as we forgive those who trespass against us, and lead us not into temptation, but deliver us from evil.

For Yours is the kingdom, and the power, and the glory, of the Father and the Son and the Holy Spirit, now and forever and to the ages of ages. Amen.

Lord, have mercy (12).

Glory to the Father and the Son and the Holy Spirit, now and forever and to the ages of ages. Amen.

O come, let us worship and bow down to our King and God.

O come, let us worship and bow down to Christ our King and God.

O come, let us worship and bow down to Christ Himself, our King and God.

PSALM 50

Prayer of Repentance

Have mercy upon me, O God, according to Your great mercy: according to the multitude of Your tender mercies blot out my iniquity. Wash me thoroughly from my iniquity, and cleanse me from my sin. For I acknowledge my iniquity: and my sin is ever before me. Against You only have I sinned, and done evil in Your sight: that You might be justified in Your words and prevail when You are judged. For behold, I was shaped in iniquity: and in sin did my mother conceive me. For behold, You have loved truth: the unclear and hidden things of Your wisdom You have made clear to me. You shall sprinkle me with hyssop, and I shall be clean: You shall wash me, and I shall be whiter than snow. You shall make me to hear joy and gladness: the bones which You have broken shall rejoice. Turn away Your face from my sins, and blot out all my iniquities. Create in me a clean heart, O God: and renew a right spirit within me. Cast me not away from Your presence: and take not Your Holy Spirit from me. Restore to me the joy of Your salvation: and steady me with a guiding spirit. Then will I teach transgressors Your ways: and the impious shall be converted to You. Deliver me from blood-guiltiness, O God, You God of my salvation: and my tongue shall sing aloud Your righteousness. O Lord, open my lips, and my mouth shall declare Your praise. For had You desired sacrifice, I would have given it You: You delight not in burnt offerings. Sacrifices to God are a contrite spirit: a contrite and humble heart, O God, You will not despise. Do good, O Lord, in Your good will to Zion: that the walls of Jerusalem may be built up. Then shall You be pleased with the sacrifices of righteousness, with burnt offering and whole burnt offerings: then shall they offer bullocks upon Your altar.

Have mercy upon us, Lord, have mercy upon us. For we sinners, void of all defense, do offer to You this petition, as to our Master; have mercy upon us.

Glory to the Father and the Son and the Holy Spirit.

Have mercy upon us, Lord, for in You have we put our trust. Be not exceedingly angry with us, nor be mindful of our iniquities, but look on us now again, for You are compassionate; and deliver us from our enemies, for You are our God and we Your people. We are all the work of Your hands, and we call on Your Name.

Now and forever and to the ages of ages. Amen.

Open unto us the door of Your compassion, Blessed Theotokos, that as we hope in You we may not fail in our petitions. May we be delivered through You from adversities, for through You has come the salvation of the Christians.

Lord, have mercy (40).

The pentitent says:

I have sinned, Lord, forgive me. God, be merciful to me, the sinner.

The priest:

Let us pray to the Lord:

O God our Savior, who by Your prophet Nathan did grant to repentant David pardon for his transgressions, and did accept Manasses's prayer of repentance: do, with Your accustomed love towards mankind, accept also Your servant (*Name*) who repents of the sins which he (*she*) has committed, overlooking all that he (*she*) hath done, pardoning

his (*her*) offenses and passing over his (*her*) sins. For You
have said, O Lord: 'With desire have I desired not the death
of a sinner, but rather that he should turn from the wickedness which he has committed, and live; and that even to
seventy times seven, sins ought to be forgiven. Since Your
majesty is incomparable, and Your mercy limitless, if You
should regard iniquity, who should stand? For You are the
God of penitents, and to You we give glory, to the Father
and the Son and the Holy Spirit, now and forever and to
the ages of ages. Amen.

Then the penitent, kneeling and with hands raised, says:

Father, Lord of heaven and earth, I confess to You all
the secret and open things of my heart and mind, which I
have done to the present day. Therefore I ask forgiveness
of You, the just and merciful judge, and grace to sin no more.

Then the priest shall say in a cheerful voice:

Brother (*Sister*), be not ashamed that you have come to
God and to me: for it is not to me that you confess, but to
God, before whom you stand.

*And the priest shall question the penitent about all his (*her*)
sins, and after a detailed examination, shall say:*

My spiritual child, who did confess to my lowliness: it
is not I, lowly and sinful, who have the power to forgive
sins upon the earth, but God. But through that divine voice
which spoke to the Apostles after the resurrection of our
Lord Jesus Christ, saying: 'If you forgive the sins of any, they
are forgiven; if you retain the sins of any, they are retained,'
taking confidence from this we also say: Whatsoever you
have confessed to my abject lowliness, and whatsoever you
did not mention, whether from ignorance or from forgetful-
ness, may God forgive you, both in the present age and in
that to come.

And he shall add the following prayer:

O God, who did forgive David the sins which he confessed through the prophet Nathan, and Peter the denial he
bitterly bewailed, and the sinful woman who wept at Your
feet, and the publican, and the prodigal son: may the same

God forgive you all through me a sinner, in this age and in that to come; and may He present you blameless before His fearful judgement-seat. Take no thought for the sins which have been forgiven you, but go in peace.

INDEX OF NAMES